PRAYER

FORMERLY TITLED
LORD, I AM WITH YOU

by
Irene Burk Harrell

LOGOS INTERNATIONAL
PLAINFIELD, NEW JERSEY

PAPERBACK EDITION—1972
Miracles Through Prayer
formerly titled
Lo, I Am With You

Acknowledgments

Acknowledgment is gratefully made to copyright holders for permission to reprint:

Scripture quotations identified as TEV: from the *Today's English Version of the New Testament.* Copyright ©American Bible Society 1966.

Scripture quotations identified as Moffatt: from *The Bible: A New Translation* by James Moffatt. Copyright, 1954 by James Moffatt. Used by permission of Harper & Row, Publishers, Inc.

Scripture quotations identified as Phillips: from *The New Testament in Modern English;* translated by J. B. Phillips. Copyright, 1958 by J. B. Phillips. Copyright, 1947, 1952, 1955 and 1957, The Macmillan Company.

Scripture quotations identified as RSV: from *The Revised Standard Version of the Bible.* Copyright, 1946 and 1952 by the Division of Christian Education of the National Council of the Churches of Christ in the United States of America.

A portion of chapter 1: from "Something to Live Up To": Reprinted by permission from *Home Life,* February 1969. Copyright ©1968, The Sunday School Board of the Southern Baptist Convention. All rights reserved. Used by permission.

A portion of chapter 2: from "Surprise Ending": Re-

More things are wrought by prayer
Than this world dreams of. Wherefore, let thy voice
Rise like a fountain for me night and day.
For what are men better than sheep or goats
That nourish a blind life within the brain,
If, knowing God, they lift not hands of prayer
Both for themselves and those who call them friends?
For so the whole round earth is every way
Bound by gold chains about the feet of God.

Alfred, Lord Tennyson:
Morte d'Arthur

Now to him who by the action of his power within us°
is able to do all, aye far more than we can ever ask or
imagine . . . EPHESIANS 3:20 (Moffatt)

° Italics mine

Table of Contents

Introduction

"None can believe how powerful prayer is, and what it is able to effect, but those who have learned it by experience."

Martin Luther said it, and, centuries later, I find myself heartily in agreement. But the experience of what prayer can do doesn't have to be my own. Others, witnessing to me about what prayer has done in their lives, have helped my faith to grow. Their witness has enabled me to venture forth, timidly — oh so timidly at first — like a baby bird reluctant to leave the known security of its limited nest, and audaciously try to fly. That I found myself, not crumpled on the ground in a broken heap, but safely landed, all in one piece, nerved me to pray again — and again.

Pascal wrote that God invented prayer to give the dignity of causality to his creatures. But it is no dignity of causality that I feel when something I have prayed for has been realized. The emotion is more like an almost delirious joy of creation, as if the lovely thing that came to pass, the thing God was yearning to do, could not have been accomplished without my help.

It is logical that the witness of people with whom you have been closely involved, persons whose lives have entered your own, will have greater impact upon your faith in prayer than witnesses which come to you by hearsay. But suppose you are not acquainted with persons of faith who can tell you of their experiences with prayer? Suppose you lack Christian friends? What then?

Fortunately for many of us, the printed word carries the intimacy of friendship. I have felt it often, a real kinship to souls whose words I read even after their bodies have long since turned to dust. Knowing this is true for me, and that books have been important in the growth of my faith, I trust the same thing may be true for you as well.

And so I offer my experiences, and some others I know well enough to believe, praying that He might use them to draw you closer to Himself.

Jesus, speaking to Peter on the very day he was to deny Him, said, "I have prayed for you, Simon, that your faith will not fail. And when you turn back to me, you must strengthen your brothers." God grant that what I have here recorded may strengthen you.

From the one man he created all races of men, and made them live over the whole earth. He himself fixed beforehand the exact times and the limits of the places where they would live. He did this so that they would look for him, and perhaps find him as they felt around for him. Yet God is actually not far from any one of us; for 'In him we live and move and are.' It is as some of your poets have also said, 'We too are his children.' ACTS 17:26-28 (TEV)

The First Step:
Mr. Pierce and Tommy

We were having a special "week of preaching" in our church. Most folks didn't want to call it a revival — they were too sophisticated for that. And some of us didn't have much in us to be revived, because we had progressed such a tiny way into His Kingdom. But our guest speaker, the Reverend Dale Fiers, not knowing our coldness, was preaching powerfully and winningly.

One night I was seated in the balcony with several of our children while my husband was singing up front with the men's choir. And the sermon was so moving, making Christ so appealing, that I almost wished I was not already a member of the church. Then I could have succumbed to the pull of the invitation hymn and given my life to Christ. But, as it was, I kept my seat.

Talking and listening on the way home that night I discovered that my husband had had a similar strong feeling. We both had to stifle an impulse to go forward. We decided to telephone some of the members of our Sunday School class. Their impulses and reactions had matched our own.

What could we do about it? It didn't occur to any of us that we ought to pray for guidance — we hadn't yet

1

learned to pray. But we considered and agreed that *IF* any of us felt the same way the next night we would not suppress our desire to go forward but would act upon it.

The night came and a more powerful sermon still, based on the 21st chapter of John. "Lovest Thou me? Then feed my sheep." A number of us went forward together to renew our pledge of faith in Him. After our own minister had greeted us and received several persons by transfer of membership he asked us to be seated in the empty front pews. Suddenly we were aware of a slight commotion near the back of the sanctuary. There came a questioning voice as a gray-haired man moved down the outside aisle.

"Is it too late? Is it too late?" he called. Then, before anyone else could speak, he answered himself with a positive affirmation: "It's not too late — it's not too late." That night Mr. Pierce made his confession of faith.

Talking with him later we learned that for years he had been yearning to join the church, yearning to publicly acknowledge his Lord but couldn't make himself do it. "I always wanted someone else to go first," he said. "I wanted someone else to go first and no one ever would."

This was the first time in our lives that we had a sense of being used by God for His high and holy purpose. It was awesome to us.

One more awesome thing happened during that week. Another night as I was sitting in the balcony, worshipping in the fullness of the Spirit that surely filled that place, I was aware of a Voice speaking to me.

"Irene, you won't have to yell at your children anymore."

Now that sounds simple enough to you but it was a

2

marvel to me. What did it mean? Did it mean that my precious (but more than occasionally lively and rowdy) children would never get through to me with their raucousity and over-indulgence in sibling rivalry? No, not at all. There would still be a normal amount of bedlam in our house but I no longer needed to be part of it. I had a new God-given serenity even when the boys' bathtime left the ceiling as splashed full of puddles as the floor. It was truly a peace that passed all understanding — a marvelous gift from God. He knew how much I needed it and I found myself being thankful to Him for the gift I hadn't prayed for.

I didn't get to keep the gift forever though. Now, I'm not implying that God took it back away from me. But I didn't take care of it. I didn't cherish it enough and use it properly. I was like a little boy with a valuable and valued new bicycle — I left it out in the rain, I failed to padlock it at night, I didn't keep the tires inflated and the screws tightened and the chain oiled. And pretty soon, because I neglected the gift, I no longer possessed it. Then I began to learn something about God's gifts — they may be free — but we have to try to live up to them.

People were always giving me presents-to-live-up-to. I first thought about it when I was fourteen. My grandmother gave me, for Christmas, a fat little red leatherette note pad with a tiny pencil attached. I put it on my bedside table and used it to make notes of things I thought about. *Wouldn't it be funny,* I mused one day, *if having this notepad turned me into a writer?*

A few years later my father gave me a new Bible. We weren't church members then, but I began to read my Bible religiously, a chapter a night before I went to bed. *Wouldn't it be something,* I thought, *if this new Bible changed my life?*

3

Years later, after I had joined the church and tried my writing wings, I was standing in our church singing the hymn of invitation. It was Mother's Day. My eldest, just turned eight, tugged at my sleeve.

"I'm going up front today, Mom," he confided in an excited whisper. I looked at him, sure he was only fooling me, and smiled back.

"Oh, Tommy, you know you're not," I assured him, wondering what had made him say such a nonsensical thing. He was just a child. He'd join later, when he was in the fifth grade or so, along with his classmates.

But Tommy meant it. "Oh, but I am — right now," and he slipped his hand out of mine and began the long walk to the front of the church.

He looked so small. And he wasn't at all the sort of child you'd expect to do such a thing on his own. His Sunday School teacher, or the preacher, must have put him up to it, I told myself. The matter-of-factness of that helped to hold back the tears as I heard him make the good confession, "I believe that Jesus is the Christ, the son of the living God, and I accept Him as my personal Saviour."

On our way home I asked him about it. "Whatever made you decide to join the church today, Tommy? Did your teacher tell you to do it?"

Tommy was still smiling and confident, pleased with himself, not shy and frowning as he was so often. "Oh, I thought it would be a good Mother's Day present for you, Mom. Something you'd like."

I had a present-to-live-up-to then, all right, a present to live up to all my life. I didn't always succeed, I failed so badly, so often. But whenever I remembered what Tommy gave me for Mother's Day, I always tried harder.

Oh Father, Lord of heaven and earth! I thank you because you have shown to the unlearned what you have hidden from the wise and learned. MATTHEW 11:25 (TEV)

The Second Step:
Virginia and 'Guerite

We had a minor disagreement in our Sunday School class one December, a blessed disagreement as it turned out, tho I didn't suspect it at the time. The subject for discussion was the taking of a Christmas "opportunity." Most of the class was in favor of providing "Santa Claus" for some impoverished family. But one woman was sufficiently affluent that she was insulated from the nature of poverty.

"Oh, let's not take a family for Christmas this year," she said, bored with the whole idea. "Everyone gets too much for Christmas. Let's wait until January or February, sometime after the first of the year, and do something for someone then. It'll mean more to them."

The rest of us didn't agree, but she wasn't the persuadable type. We felt that our only choice was to go along with her to avoid a fuss. Inwardly we resolved to make the most of whatever opportunity we took later, working with them throughout the year, to prove that Christian kindness was not a one-time Christmas fling but an enduring caring for our brothers.

I suppose we intended to begin in January, but we didn't. There is about Christmas something that gives

7

a special impetus to love that is lacking the rest of the time. And so, not surprisingly, we never made the beginning at all.

But as we approached the next Christmas season, the dissenting member of the class had moved away and the rest of us made ambitious plans, plans that, carried out, were to have a major impact on our lives.

From the Salvation Army list in the evening paper we chose a family composed of a mother and four small children. A telephone call brought information about the family's circumstances. The mother was twenty-four and her four children were Arthur Lee, 8, Violet, 5, Danny, 3, and David Ray, 8 months old.

Income? The family lived in the country, rent-free. The mother made a little money working in tobacco during the summer. And she had a year-round house-cleaning job on Friday mornings. It paid her two dollars a week.

The family was eligible for surplus foods from the government. Before 1965 the woman had earned enough in the summer to eke out an existence for herself and her brood. But recently major surgery for her had interfered. Their situation sounded desperate.

"We ought to go out to see the mother," I told my husband, "and find out what they need most."

And so, on a cold Saturday afternoon before Christmas we drove out of town to the second of five little "endway" houses where our "opportunity" lived.

I remember turning up the collar of my coat against a near-freezing wind as we stepped from our warm station wagon into the bare dirt of the front yard. No smoke came from the chimney and I was sure there would be no one at home, but we climbed the detached cement stairs to the front door and knocked.

There was no knob on the door, only a hole where a knob might have been, once. The window panes had

8

rags stuffed in the cracks. Several broken-out panes were supplanted by cardboard from cereal boxes. There was no screen or storm door, but I wasn't surprised at that. I had passed poor colored houses in the country and was used to the look of the outside of them. But I'd never been inside one before.

At our knock a voice called out, "Who is it?" When we had identified ourselves, the rag of plastic curtain at the window moved a little and a small brown face just high enough to see through peeked out.

After a minute the door was opened by the eight-year-old boy. He had on a shirt, of sorts, something that passed for pants, and nothing else.

"Is your mother at home?" I asked. "We want to see her."

"Mama not home," he announced gravely. "She workin'."

"Well, is any grownup here with you?" He shook his head.

My husband, just behind me on the steps, suggested, "Let's step in for a minute. The house'll get cold with the door standing open." Arthur Lee moved back and we entered the room.

I'll never forget what we saw. To our left was what purported to be a bed. The mattress, filthy and sagging almost to the floor, oozed stuffing at every rip and seam. There were no sheets, only a pile of dirty rags for cover. In the corner was a small chest of drawers. Its top held a dusty glass punch bowl with cups hanging around the rim. A white Bible lay beside it.

In the middle of the wall facing the door stood a small black wood-stove, long since cold because there was no fuel to keep the fire going. Beside the stove, on the floor, was a chipped enamel pan with some cold remains of corn meal mush the children had been eating by fistfuls.

9

The children? Oh yes, the children. The eight year old who let us in stood beside a little sister and a younger brother, both barefoot and hardly clothed. Violet's dress had the bodice held to the skirt by a large safety pin.

And then I saw the baby. At first I thought he was lying on a pile of straw. But the straw was what had once been an upholstered chair, only the upholstery was gone, now. The baby wore a rag of undershirt and a diaper that hadn't been changed or washed for a long time. Where the shirt and diaper parted there was an umbilical hernia as big as an orange. As I looked at the baby he smiled at me, happily gnawing on a greasy little square of bristly hog skin.

I thought of my own baby in her lovely birch crib with its clean white sheets. I remember saying, "Oh, Daddy," before I started to cry.

When I could see again I took a piece of paper from my pocket and laid it on the floor, kneeling beside it. We had wanted to find out what sizes the children wore, but sizes seemed superfluous now. I could see that just any size clothing would do, just so it was clothing. Shoes were a little different, though, and I asked the three older children to let me see how big their feet were. There was a lot of shuffling and hiding behind one another before Arthur Lee came bravely forward and put his foot on the paper so I could draw around it. Violet and Danny were next, giggling when my pencil touched their feet.

That afternoon, when we came back with blankets, shoes, diapers, food and clothes, the mother was gone again. We could tell she'd been at home because the fire was blazing so hot the children had the front door standing wide open. A coal scuttle was full of scraps of linoleum torn from debris piled in the yard next door. It made a fire that seemed dangerously hot for such a ramshackle dwelling.

10

We saw the rest of the house that day. The second room held a broken-down daybed and a mirrored wardrobe. The kitchen had a small gas stove and a table. There were no chairs. There was no sink, no water. The mother carried all water for washing and drinking and cooking from a yard pump a couple of houses away.

I wondered if we would ever find the mother at home so we could talk to her. Arthur Lee told us that on school days five-year-old Violet took care of the three year old and the baby if his mother was able to get work.

The next afternoon the house was packed with a curious crowd when we arrived. The mother was among them. Because there wasn't room for us in the house, Virginia came out to sit in the car with us. She was a tiny thing in a bouffant yellow organdy dress. Polite when we talked to her, she answered our questions and seemed not offended that we had come to help.

Yes, she would be home the day before Christmas if we came to bring some things. What did she need most? Well, a refrigerator so the baby's bottle of milk wouldn't sour so fast. And some warm cover for the bed. And something to burn in the stove.

The class found a refrigerator, a bed, a crib for the baby, several chairs for the kitchen and some sheets for the new bed. There were toys for the children, new clothes for everyone and food. The wood stove was replaced with an oil stove that would not go out when the mother was away. The class had decided to pay oil bills for the year.

Our "opportunity's" immediate physical needs were relatively easy to take care of. But I was discouraged. How could we ever make a real difference in their lives?

11

"How on earth do you reach someone like that?" I had asked despairingly, time after time when we had just met Virginia and her children. "Everything about us is so different, we'll never be able to make a dent. We'll never even get to know one another, really."

But we did get to know, and love, Virginia and her children. Every week or two we'd go to see them, carrying with us hand-me-downs or groceries or books to read — and sometimes only friendship.

Gradually what had seemed impossible in the beginning came to be. After a while Virginia was not strange-looking to me anymore. She was actually pretty, poised, intelligent and witty. She always seemed glad to see us, even when we went empty-handed. I remember the pride with which she asked me to sit down in one of her chairs one day. She hadn't been able to exercise that kind of courtesy before, when she'd had no chairs.

I'd been pleased to learn that Virginia didn't smoke or drink and that she actually read her Bible. So I was quite taken aback the day she opened the door and spat into the yard while we were talking. It was then I realized that the peculiar swelling I noticed sometimes on the side of her face was the snuff of which she partook regularly.

"Virginia," I said, "someday I'm going to ask you to do something for me." I had in mind that I'd ask her to give up dipping snuff, and I'd explain that she was much too pretty to spoil her face with it.

"Oh," she replied, "it doesn't matter what you ask me to do — I'll do anything for you."

The important thing Virginia was to do for me neither of us knew then. She was probably thinking in terms of ironing, washing windows or scrubbing floors. And I was thinking in terms of her giving up a trivial habit that offended me.

12

"Someday I want to see where you live," Virginia told me. She had become just as interested in us and in our children as we were in her. And one day she came. I showed her around the house and let her wash a window for me before I gave her some lunch.

Virginia wanted to wash all of my windows — they needed it — and came back several days that week and the next to finish them. She did a perfect job, scraping off all the little drops of paint I had let remain for five years. My windows shone. I had a brighter view of the world outside.

Virginia sang while she worked. Things were "looking up" for her. The children had clothing now and she was receiving a monthly welfare check and a small support payment from the father of her children. She was able to find some "day work" and the baby was taking iron to build up his hemoglobin for surgery to reduce his hernia. Virginia had even had a proposal of marriage from a young man in her church. He had said that he would love her children as if they were his own. Virginia had promised to give him an answer within a month, after she had a chance to pray about it.

Our "opportunity" prayed about other things, too. One morning she came in especially full of talk. As usual she greeted our baby girl, getting down on the floor to talk to her. When she had finished she stood up abruptly. Her words poured out in a torrent of sincerity and love.

"Oh, Miz Harrell," she said, "I believe that 'Guerite is gonna be able to hear. Don't you believe she is? Can't she already hear a lot better than she could? Oh, Miz Harrell, I been prayin' about your baby, that God would heal her, ever since you first tole me about her trouble. I just *know* she gonna hear!"

13

Our baby, just a few months older than hers, was a "rubella baby." German measles during my pregnancy had left her profoundly deaf.

'Guerite was nearly twelve months old that Christmas when we first began to notice a change in her. She began responding to some sounds that had not reached her before. By the end of March, when we took her back to the University Hearing Clinic for further testing, there was no doubt in our minds. Our daughter, whose nerve deafness had been pronounced complete and incurable, had begun to hear a little.

The doctors were amazed, but Virginia wasn't even surprised. "I knowed it, Miz Harrell. Didn't I tell you I knowed it? Prayer works, just like the Bible say it do. I gonna keep on prayin' for your baby."

I had been wrong about the gulf between Virginia and me. It was an artificial one. There was an easy meeting ground between us when we encountered what really mattered. Our differences disappeared when we talked of God and of prayer and of what we wished for our children.

It didn't matter that Virginia had quit school in the ninth grade and that I had degrees from two universities. It didn't matter that her house had no bathroom and mine had several. It didn't matter that Virginia had no husband while I was married to the Judge. It didn't matter that her church met in an unpainted shanty and mine met in a Gothic cathedral. We were both children of the same God. And Virginia's faith was teaching mine.

Of course I had prayed for our child too. But my prayers had been prayers of thankfulness for her, not prayers for her healing. I was too scientific for that. I had to see a miracle to believe it.

When I reached for my purse to pay her for washing windows, Virginia protested. She didn't want to take

14

money for doing them, she said. She wanted to do something for me, since I had done so much for her.

I? So much for her? But think what her faith had done for me!

"That won't do, Virginia," I'd told her. "I'm glad to pay you for washing windows. There are so many things your children need that money can buy. Here, take it." I pressed the money into her hand. I had inquired around and learned the "going rate" for washing windows.

But then I stopped. I could pay Virginia for a little thing like washing windows, but how could I pay her for the important thing she had done for me? How could I pay her whose faithful prayers had been a part of God's plan for restoring hearing to my child? What would be the "going rate" for that?

There seemed at first no satisfactory answer. *Oh,* I said to myself, *you're just being silly. Of course you can't pay someone for praying for your child.*

But then it came to me. The truth of it came home. I *could* pay Virginia for praying for my child. Not just could — but had to — must!

Only I couldn't pay her in money that tarnishes or in things that wear out. I would have to pay Virginia for her prayers for me and my child by getting on my knees to pray for Virginia and her child.

Did I call it a Christmas opportunity? Well, it began with Christmas. But it lasts forever.

That Virginia's prayers helped our faith — and the faith of others to whom we witnessed — to grow was not the end of it. Our church, having just completed a new educational building alongside the sanctuary, found itself in need of a bigger custodial staff. Could Virginia be trained to serve there?

Today Virginia lives in a neat little house with rocking chairs on a front porch, shrubbery around the lawn, and an automatic washer in the kitchen. There's a bathroom with a hot water heater and a tub. The baby who had the hernia is a happy tricycling toddler, his surgery successfully over. The young man who proposed to Virginia didn't turn out to be the right one — her prayers for guidance in her decision were unmistakably answered one morning when she encountered him uptown — drunk. She has been working full-time as an indispensable maid and nursery helper in our church for over three years now.

And, in the summer of 1969, Virginia walked down the aisle in a long ivory satin and lace wedding gown to become Mrs. Cornelius Lewis. One night Cornelius came to our home with Virginia. He played his electric guitar while she stood beside him, her hands clasped in front of her, and sang about her Jesus. No Metropolitan opera performance could have warmed my heart more.

Virginia told me once that she thought she'd like to go back to school to finish her high school education. We talked about that for a little, and then I asked her what else she wanted to do with her life, if the way didn't open for her to continue her schooling.

"Well," she said, "I just want to take care of my children and serve the Lord wherever I am."

Serve the Lord. I thought about how she had served Him already, about how she had taught me about prayer. And, because of Virginia, I had become more aware of trying to serve Him too.

One day Peter and John went to the Temple at three o'clock in the afternoon, the hour for prayers. There, at the "Beautiful Gate," as it was called, was a man who had been lame all his life. Every day he was carried to this gate to beg for money from the people who were going into the Temple. When he saw Peter and John going in, he begged them to give him something. They looked straight at him and Peter said, "Look at us!" So he looked at them, expecting to get something from them. ACTS 3:1-5 (TEV)

Then Peter said, Silver and gold have I none; but such as I have give I thee. In the name of Jesus Christ of Nazareth rise up and walk. And he took him by the right hand, and lifted him up: and immediately his feet and ankle bones received strength. And he leaping up stood, and walked, and entered with them into the temple, walking, and leaping, and praising God. ACTS 3:6-9 (KJV)

The Third Step:
Maizie and Me

Our lives had been so wonderfully blessed by our experience with Virginia that we knew any future "opportunities" "adopted" by our Sunday School class would be anticlimactic for us. There could be significant blessings for someone else however, someone who'd not been "involved" before. For that reason, and because our lives were already so full of a number of things, Allen and I decided that some other members of the class ought to make the initial contact with an opportunity family in 1966 and provide the continuing link of friendship. But somehow it didn't work out quite as we planned it.

Allen and I were with the group that made the first pre-Christmas visit to a woman whose husband was in prison. She had three small children and no income, but, because she lived with her brother, was able to keep the children fed and clothed.

There was a bed in the corner of the large but sparsely furnished front room. In the dim light provided by a naked bulb hanging from the ceiling I made out the figure of a woman lying under the covers. She seemed to me to be old, and very sick. But we didn't pay much attention. After all, she wasn't our "opportunity." The woman who took care of her was. We

19

found out what the little ones wanted for Christmas and returned to our comfortable homes.

After Christmas it fell our lot to visit the family again. The same woman was lying on the bed still and we asked a few questions about her. Her name was Maizie, she was 22 years old, had a five-year-old daughter and was confined to her bed because she was paralyzed from the waist down!

Being still more scientific than spiritual, our first impulse was to see what medical assistance was available for her. Soon we learned the heartbreaking news from specialists at a famed university hospital. Maizie was born with a malformation of blood vessels in her spine. There was an area where rushing arterial blood flowed directly into a knotted mass of thin-walled veins. The mass, like a tangled snarl of rubber bands, was down inside the spinal column where no surgery could reach it.

The malformation had ballooned when Maizie was expecting her second child, and began pressing on vital nerves, causing her to drag one leg. A therapeutic abortion had been performed to prolong Maizie's life, and, for a while, she had walked normally. But slowly and inevitably the tangled area ballooned again, larger and larger, until, in November of 1966, Maizie was bed-ridden, unable to walk, unable to take care of her family or herself.

Doctors explained to us that Maizie would never walk again, that the paralysis would increase until it affected some vital organ and she would die. It wouldn't take long. They had seen other patients like her. The prognosis was always the same. Hopeless. The marvels of modern medicine could do nothing.

There was nothing we could do either. Or was there? It couldn't hurt to pray.

And we did pray for Maizie, and asked our friends

to pray, that God's will would be done in her life. We had no idea what His will might be.

For a while after we began to pray for Maizie she seemed to get worse. The paralysis that had affected the lower part of her body crept into her hands and arms, depriving them of strength. Her hands were drawn, the fingers curved in, like claws, toward her palms. She spent most of her time in bed, sitting up in a chair when someone carried her to it. Her legs never moved unless someone moved them for her, or when the paralysis caused them to jump spasmodically, uncontrollably, kicking into the air.

We went to see Maizie every few weeks. We told her about our little girl, whose hearing had improved remarkably after people had prayed for her. We told her about a woman who had been healed of an incurable cancer after she had an experience of Christ. We believed that sometimes God healed people whose ailments were medically incurable. *Maybe* it would be His will for her to be healed. Maybe. We didn't tell her how impossible her case was. We didn't know then that nothing is impossible with God.

One day I prayed *with* Maizie, my hands on her cold, thin, lifeless legs. I don't remember the words I said. But I do remember that I was still in the dark about God's will for her. Was it His will for her to suffer and die, letting someone be redeemed by the faith and uncomplaining courage with which she bore her affliction? Or was it His will for her to live, for the paralysis to be arrested? I didn't dream that it could be taken away.

Maizie's legs were wet with my tears when we finished our prayer. Were her legs warmer than they had been before? Or was it only my imagination? My heart was leaden but I tried to encourage Maizie to believe that she was already being healed, above all

21

she could ask or think. And I told her to give thanks in all things and for all things — even for pain. But I wasn't thankful yet myself.

On a particularly dreary day we found Maizie lying across the bed, so thin she seemed almost bodiless beneath the blanket. Her eyes were matted, swollen almost shut with sores. My diary entry was bleak. "Maizie is not long for this world."

In November, a year after Maizie's paralysis had put her to bed to stay, some friends went with us to an Episcopal healing service. I was planning to go to the communion rail for the laying on of hands in behalf of someone. Who should it be? Should I go for a friend, horribly crippled with arthritis? Should I go for my still-hard-of-hearing child? Should I go for another person on my prayer list?

Maizie's name didn't enter my mind until I rose to go forward, still undecided. Then I heard, clear as a spoken word, "There is still *time* for them. Go for Maizie!" And so I knelt for her as the minister laid his hands on my head and pronounced the words of the sacrament.

I sent Maizie's name to several prayer groups so they could add their intercessions to ours. And I took her to the prayer group of which I had become a member. All of them prayed for Maizie — so did many others, including faithful members of her own family, and a woman preacher, said to have the gift of healing.

There were prayers and more prayers. But how would they be answered? One night, in January of 1968, the telephone rang about eleven o'clock. I recognized the voice immediately. It was Frances, Maizie's sister, and she sounded excited and out of breath.

"Miz Harrell! Miz Harrell!" And she told me that Maizie had asked for a pencil and had been able to grasp it and to write her name! That was news! Her hands had been *so* weak. But they hadn't been paralyzed. So it didn't sound like any miracle to me.

We asked Maizie to shake hands with us when we went to see her a few days later. And her grip was surprisingly strong. She seemed in better spirits too. We planned to take her some yarn and some knitting needles to help her pass the time. Maybe she'd be able to sell some of her knitting and help earn a living even tho she would still be an invalid the rest of her life.

As we were visiting Maizie one day I asked her, "Is there anything you need, anything we can bring you the next time we come?" Her sagging bed, worn linoleum, the ragged curtains — all spoke eloquently of need.

But Maizie shook her head. "No," she said, "no, I don't need anything."

Her mother-in-law, standing in the doorway, laughed. "Oh yes you do, Maizie Lee," she said. "You need money."

I laughed too, thinking of how little money we had. And I started to quote some scripture to her: "Silver and ggold have I none —" and then I stopped abruptly. I knew the rest of what Peter said, but I couldn't say it. I couldn't say, "Silver and gold have I none, but such as I have give I thee; In the name of Jesus Christ of Nazareth, rise up and walk."

No, I couldn't say that. I didn't have that kind of faith to give. Not at all. I had still only a smidgen of faith in prayer — all I had been able to receive out of the bounty He offered. But I had been blessed with an abundant love for her whom I saw so sorely afflicted. So instead of telling Maizie to get up and walk we took her a wheelchair on our next trip. That was a valid commentary on the strength of my faith — *it* needed a wheelchair.

And then something happened. It was close to midnight when the phone rang this time. I lifted the receiver and heard heavy breathing — as if someone had run to the telephone.

"Miz Harrell?" The voice at the other end took a deep breath. "This is Frances. Maizie moved her leg. She wanted me to call you."

My husband saw the look on my face as I cradled the receiver. "What was that about? Bad news?"

Speechless for an instant I could only shake my head. But my mind raced, arguing.

Maizie *couldn't* have moved her leg. She was paralyzed from the waist down, and had been ever since we'd met her.

My mind came back to the present when I became aware of my husband's questioning look.

"That was Maizie's sister," I told him. "She said that Maizie moved her leg."

We looked at each other incredulously for a moment. The next day we went to see Maizie. She was sitting in a chair with both feet on the floor when we arrived. After we had visited for a while I asked if she wanted to move her leg for us. Her face mirrored great concentration and tremendous effort as she lifted her right foot a scant inch from the floor and wiggled it back and forth in a tiny arc. It was weak, so very weak, but it wasn't paralyzed!

What rejoicing there was that day in that house and in our own! As the weeks passed we all prayed with new faith, new fervour and overflowing thanksgiving. Maizie's leg grew stronger until one day she was able to cross her right leg over her still lifeless left one. We took her back to the doctor then — not for treatment, but so that he could see and believe. When she crossed her legs he grabbed his reflex hammer off the shelf, testing her reactions with it. He was impressed. "Very

24

unusual, for function to be restored like that," he admitted. And he kept shaking his head.

When we left the clinic my purse was loaded down with vitamin pills and appetite tonic for Maizie to take. An orderly lifted her into her wheelchair and rolled her to my car in the parking lot.

After that Maizie grew stronger day by day. Soon she could move her left leg. Supported on both sides, she took one step, then two. A faith-filled friend brought a light-weight walker for her to use. At first the walker stood in the corner of the room while Maizie got about in her wheelchair. Then she tried standing up in the walker, a few minutes at a time. She began to help in the kitchen, preparing meals and washing the dishes by herself. It was quite a change from being helpless, being able to help others.

Maizie's left leg was still rather draggy. Thinking out loud at home I said, "Maybe the doctor could put a brace on that leg. It might help." Tommy, my son, shot me a withering glance.

"A brace, Mom? Are you crazy? That'd be like a crutch! God's going to make her *well!*" And my son was right.

In August I took Maizie to the doctor again. As she made her way down the long hall of the clinic, pushing her walker frame ahead of her, I was surprised to see the frame tip at a sharp angle. I was afraid Maizie was going to fall. But she laughed when I stared.

"See, I can walk all by myself now," she said. "I can carry the walker part of the time instead of having it carry me."

Before long Maizie graduated from her walker. She no longer needed any support — except the Lord.

One morning I was with Maizie at the hospital where we had gone for physical therapy to help "educate" her new walk to eliminate a slight limp. Maizie's doctor was there, explaining her case to the therapist. The therapist was plainly dumfounded.

"You don't mean to tell me that that girl, walking down the hallway by herself, is the same girl as the one whose x-rays you were telling me about? It just *can't* be!"

Her doctor nodded. "I know," he said. "It can't be — but it is."

I was thinking about it a different way. The therapist was right — the Maizie who walked down the hall wasn't the same Maizie. She wasn't the Maizie who had lain so long and so sick and so motionless in bed. Hadn't He told us, "Behold, I make all things new"? And Maizie *was* made new. I had seen newness fulfilled in her. I had seen wholeness born out of brokenness.

The doctor's word that day was, "Amazing, simply amazing!" Doctors don't say "miracle" much. But at least one of them has seen that "incurable" doesn't mean "hopeless" at all. It just means that hope has to be in the Lord.

And Maizie's walking wasn't the only miracle. I saw another one at the same time. God had taken my weak faith — a faith that needed a wheelchair — and made it whole.

Ask, and you will receive; seek, and you will find; knock, and the door will be opened to you. For everyone who asks will receive, and he who seeks will find, and the door will be opened to him who knocks. Would any one of you fathers give his son a stone, when he asks you for bread? Or would you give him a snake, when he asks for fish? As bad as you are, you know how to give good things to your children. How much more, then, your father in heaven will give good things to those who ask him! MATTHEW 7:7-11 (TEV)

"Lo, I am with you always." MATTHEW 28:20 (RSV)

The Fourth Step:
All Things Made New

While the big miracles of 'Guerite and Maizie were
taking place around us, as answers to prayer, we became increasingly conscious of God's power at work in
the dailiness of our lives as well.

It all began one night when I reached rock bottom. I
wasn't aware of God's power at work in my life at all
just then — but of myself working and working and
working, from early morning until late at night and
never finishing with laundry and cooking and cleaning
and gardening and entertaining and settling the children's interminable quarrels and hearing other people's problems poured out to me for endless hours on
the telephone.

Life, which should have been beautiful, was becoming unbearably gruesome. And *I* was the worst part of
it, impossible to live with, tired of living. I was supposed to be strong enough to take it all. But I wasn't.
His strength was not in me—I'd never really invited
it, whole-heartedly, except for emergencies. Now my
whole existence had become an emergency, a life-or-
death matter. One night, overcome with the hopelessness of it all, and my own utter failure and help-
lessness, I was driven to my knees. How the tears
flowed as kneeling by our bed my husband and I

poured out our confessions, our supplications, a new total commitment and finally, our thanksgiving for His help.

It was July 13, 1967, and life has had a new dimension ever since.

We didn't know what had happened to us. But something had, and we needed to share it. I remember telling some friends that I had just been converted. They looked at me as if they thought I was crazy.

"Converted? But, Irene, you've been active in the church for years—" They didn't understand what I was talking about. I didn't know the words for it then. I'd never heard of the baptism of the Holy Spirit. But I did know that I was different—there was a peace in me and around me that I had not known before.

The next morning I was up early, to read my Bible. It had been such a dull book during much of my life. I had an English professor once who had pointed out to his class some of the beautiful passages of the King James' version. And I'd often wished I could find my old notes to refresh my memory about where the beautiful passages were to be found. I'd never had much luck looking for the beautiful passages on my own.

But suddenly that was different too. On the first morning of my new life I was led to read the first chapter of Ecclesiastes. I saw there how there is nothing new under the sun but such weariness as man cannot utter. That described my condition exactly—my former condition, that is.

And then I turned to one remembered verse in Revelation, "Behold, I make all things new," and I claimed its promise for myself.

Every morning I copied scripture after scripture in my notebook—all of it so beautiful and so true and so personally meaningful it was as if I was reading even relatively familiar passages for the first time in my life. My eyes, my ears, my life, were opened.

In the same notebook I wrote down my morning prayer:

"Oh Lord, I thank Thee that Thou hast made me new, as if the past self of despisings and frustrations and ugliness had never been, it had been washed so clean. Leave no contagion there to reinfect me with willfulness and stubbornness and criticalness and wanting to have my own way about things.

"Bless all I love this day and make me love Thee more than any other. Use me to serve Thy little ones. Let it not be too late for me to make amends to my children . . ."

Oh, there was still a lot of work for me to do, but it wasn't burdensome any longer. "My yoke is easy, my burden light." It was all joy—because I was privileged to do everything for Him.

Every morning I recorded page after page of intercessions, of thanksgiving, of joy.

On the second day—

"Keep me to Thee in it, in all the doings of this day, as Thou didst keep me yesterday. Let no evil befall me or those I love. Let no temptation of frustration or anger come near me. Take away even my unspoken impatience and help me to see that it is I who need to change rather than anyone else, for Thy sake. Let me have a proper sense of priorities—let me put the most important things ahead of the conventionally respectable ones.

"I embrace Thy healing forgiveness for all the times I have let blessings be as curses to my soul. Let me know that when I hate anyone or any *thing,* I am hating Thee. Let me hate only evil, and that, not because it affronts my sensibilities, but because it is an affront to Thee.

"Ever bless and keep in Thy loving care all those we love—and let our love encompass all the earth. For Jesus' sake."

31

On the third day—

"Accept my prayer of thanksgiving for this, another clean new day with the mist of Thy Holy Spirit veiling and bathing the whole outdoors where I hear a mourning dove calling—and a cheering quail. I thank Thee for the shining newness in my soul.

> Let me love, this day,
>   in a richer, fuller way.
> Let my every action be
>   a faithful witness unto Thee."

And beautiful scripture? It was everywhere I looked!

"Blessed is the man . . . (whose) delight is in the law of the Lord." Psalms 1:1-2 (KJV) "Blessed are all who take refuge in him." Psalms 2:12 (RSV)

"Oh Lord, I thank You that I know the happiness of one who delights in the law of the Lord, who finds refuge in Him. I thank You that You have commanded us to love one another and that even now You are working in my heart to change any unconsciously harbored hates to outgoing love."

"Let the heavens be glad, and let the earth rejoice; let the sea roar, and all that fills it; let the field exult and everything in it!" Psalms 96:11-12 (RSV)

"But I through the abundance of thy steadfast love will enter thy house." Psalms 5:7 (RSV)

"Oh Lord, give me to know that I will enter Thy house through the abundance of Thy steadfast love, and not through any small virtue of my own (which never is mine, but Thine on me bestowed by Thy mercy and grace). Take away my sins and make me as I ought to be: patient, loving, kind. Let me receive every ordinary frustration as an opportunity to serve Thee."

32

"Oh Lord, our Lord, how majestic is thy name in all the earth!" Psalms 8:1 (RSV)

How majestic indeed! And another morning, in the midst of all the newness, all the glory, I asked:

"Lord, I pray that You will use my writing to turn others to Thee, that the witness I can give of the change in my life will make a door where Your Holy Spirit can enter into a man and take away his lostness, restoring him to Thee. Guide now my pen, my hand, my life, to Thy glory. In Jesus' name I ask it."

"I love thee, O Lord, my strength. Make me to know thy ways, O Lord; teach me thy paths. Lead me in thy truth, and teach me, for thou art the God of my salvation; for thee I wait all the day long." Psalms 18:1; 25:4; 25:5 (RSV)

"Oh, yes, Lord! In Thee is my strength. I would know Thy truth and, even when I do not understand it, I would be *willingly* led in it.

"Thou knowest that my willing has been a passive thing. Accept now my *positive, active* willingness. I am *willing,* with the strength of the Lord that is in me, to be Thy servant, to spend my life in love serving Thee, serving Thy little ones for Thy sake."

A few weeks later we spent a day at the river.

"Oh Lord, I thank You that this is such a happy, such a blessed spot—not because the water and sand and sky and happy children are beautiful, but because You are here in the midst of us. Let it be ever so, that in the midst of joy or sorrow I will recognize and claim Thy presence for my peace."

My sacrifice—all I had to give—a broken spirit, a broken and contrite heart, had been acceptable to Him. And He had rewarded me.

"I am continually with thee; thou dost hold my right hand. Thou dost guide me with thy counsel, and afterward thou wilt receive me to glory. Whom have I in heaven but thee? And there is nothing upon earth that I desire besides thee. My flesh and my heart may fail, but God is the strength of my heart and my portion forever." Psalms 73:23-26 (RSV)

What more could I want, having His presence, His guidance, His promise of life eternal with Him?

It was enough.

"O sing to the Lord a new song, for he has done marvelous things!" Psalm 98:1 (RSV)

And He keeps on doing them—

There was, for instance, the Sunday when we learned the truth of Matthew 6:8 (TEV) "God is your Father and he already knows what you need before you ask him."

I wasn't being exactly honest with God in my impromptu prayers in our Sunday School class that morning. "You alone know the needs of each one here," I prayed. "Guide and guard us thru this day, supplying our every need. In Jesus' name, Amen."

These were the words I said, but inwardly I was acknowledging that I, too, knew the needs of our class members. There was Bill—he had just lost his job and needed faith and courage while he looked for a new one. There was Sarah, pregnant, needing good health and confidence so she could carry this baby to full term and not lose it as she had several others. There was Tom, in the middle of divorce proceedings. He certainly needed an awareness of God's comforting presence. There I was, needing a clear strong voice and untrembling knees to deliver the Woman's Day sermon in church later in the morning.

Oh, I believed that God knew the needs of His people, all right. But didn't I know them too? Not quite all of them, as it turned out later, when my prayer was answered above all I could ask or think.

34

After church we loaded our six kids into the car and drove ninety miles to Chapel Hill to visit our beloved Aunt Myrt. Noticing the declining needle on the gas gauge, my husband said, "Oh, shucks! We'll have to get gas before we get home tonight. I meant to have Charlie fill the tank yesterday, but forgot all about it."

The gasoline situation wasn't critical just then so we didn't stop. We didn't even think about gas again until a few minutes after nine that night when we were cruising down the superhighway after our afternoon of visiting. We'd headed for home an hour earlier than usual. I didn't even wonder about why, but the kids did.

"Aw, Mom," Tom had pleaded when I told them to get their things together to head for home. "We never go this early. Why can't we stay another hour? We always do." I just shook my head. It *was* early but my husband and I were both ready to go so we got the kids into the car, hugged Aunt Myrt goodbye and backed out of the drive.

There was a lot of traffic. *Superhighways are scary things,* I thought, *especially if you happen to have car trouble.* I gave an involuntary shudder as a car flew past us and barely missed another pulling out of our lane just ahead. I'd surely be glad to get home!

Just then our car made a funny coughing sound, and the motor strained.

"What the—" my husband exclaimed, hitting the brakes. "Something's wrong." He looked completely mystified. "I've never had it act like that before."

We were at exactly the right place to take advantage of an opening in the median strip and cross the other lanes to the lone service station on a hilltop directly across the road.

"Oh, I'd forgotten about the gas," I said. "We never got any, did we? Could that be it?"

The children, who had been holding their breaths in apprehension, exhaled smiling as we pulled up along-side the filling station pump. Before my husband could turn off the ignition the motor died and couldn't be revived. No earthly engineer could have calculated our fuel needs so exactly.

When the attendant came out to help us, we all watched the changing numerals on the dial of the pump . . . 16, 17, 18, 18.4 the numbers read when the pump turned off.

"How much does the tank hold?" Alice wanted to know.

"Eighteen gallons," her Daddy answered as he stepped on the accelerator and was rewarded with the sound of a car ready to go.

"Eighteen gallons?" James and Susan chimed in. "But he put in almost eighteen and a half!"

"I know, I know," their Daddy nodded, "because that's how much we needed this time. And there's something else, too," he told them. "Remember how you kids fussed because we left an hour early? For no good reason? Well, that station would have been closed for the night if we'd come along an hour later."

I thought then about my impromptu prayer. And how God had answered it with promptings to us to leave early, and promptings to the car to act peculiar at exactly the right spot. He *had* known some needs I wasn't aware of, after all.

We checked the speedometer as we drove off. There wasn't another open-for-business gas station for the next four miles. Our singing the rest of that trip con-sisted mainly of swelling choruses of "God will take care of you." He had just shown us how.

Running out of gasoline could have been merely a minor inconvenience, of course. But last Valentine's Day we found His help in a situation that involved a matter of life or death.

My husband and I were celebrating with Ralph and Ann, some dear friends. We had gone to an extra-special steak house for supper, had enjoyed enormous salads, and were ready to begin on the sizzling steaks that had just been delivered to our table.

Ralph, being a preacher, suggested that my husband ask the blessing, and he did, praying that the food would nourish our bodies and that our fellowship together would nourish our souls. None of us could have guessed how vital that fellowship was about to be for him.

Conversation ceased momentarily as we picked up knives and forks and prepared to try our steaks. My husband was hungry. Lunch, for him, had been a long time ago, in the middle of a full day in court, a day with a long criminal docket.

After one bite proved that his ribeye was both tender and delicious he put his fork into a piece of baked potato and raised it to his mouth. Then it happened.

Somehow a piece of scratchy potato peeling didn't go down right but lodged itself in his windpipe. At first he thought a little coughing would clear it. But he didn't seem to have any air to cough *with*. He had been choked before, and while the experience had never been particularly pleasant, it had never been serious either. This was different.

He couldn't cough. His air was gone. His chest ached. His throat was closed. I was aware of peculiar agonizing sounds coming from his chest as he struggled for breath.

People do die from choking on food. The thought entered my mind and clung there. *People do die—*

Would he die? His desperate struggle for breath was futile. Was there a doctor in the restaurant—*anyone* who could perform a tracheotomy so he could breathe again? They'd have to do it right away. He was about gone.

I could see Ann's face, and Ralph's. They seemed to be yearning with concern for him—and with fright—as they looked on helplessly. Would *they* do something before it was too late?

One thought kept running through my mind in the midst of all of this. It was a motto I had read just that week in a book by E. Stanley Jones. The motto was, "Not my responsibility, but my response to His ability."

It seemed appropriate time to call on His ability. Strangely calm, I laid my hand lightly on my husband's arm, bowed my head and, silently, prayed. As I closed my eyes, I was flooded with the certainty that although *I* didn't know what to do, Jesus *did* know, and would provide the help my husband needed if I would ask Him. And so I asked, trusting. And then I thanked Him and looked up.

Suddenly my husband was perfectly all right. He was breathing naturally. But there was a strange look on his face. Exactly what had happened?

My husband explained. "I knew you were praying," he said softly. "And while you were praying I heard the Voice."

"The voice?" we asked, almost in unison. None of us heard anything except the sounds of his agony.

"Yes," he nodded. "I heard the Voice. In another second I could not have heard it, could not have obeyed it.

"The instructions were perfectly clear.

" 'Breathe out what you have. Breathe out what you have,' "I had been struggling to breathe in, all my instincts screaming for an intake of air. How could I breathe out?

38

"But the Voice was clear. And it was to be obeyed. With a mighty effort of will I breathed out the tiny bit of air that had collected in my lungs.

"Immediately my windpipe was freed from the obstruction. The offending potato peel was moved aside. I could breathe again. I'm going to be all right."

And he was *so* completely all right that I felt it necessary to touch his arm again, this time with a slight restraining pressure as he speared another big chunk of potato with his fork and began to raise it to his mouth.

"Don't you think it might be a good idea to wait just a little," I chided, "and let your throat rest a minute?"

We all had to laugh at his eagerness to dive in and rejoiced at the fact that he'd had no ill effects at all from his close brush with suffocation.

As we rode home that night we rejoiced in God's goodness, in his "very present help in trouble."

And we shared a dramatically new understanding of how necessary it is to be obedient to God's voice, giving Him everything we have—to the last breath—in order that we might receive the blessings He has for us.

"Behold, I will cause breath to enter you, and ye shall live." Ezekiel 37:5 (KJV)

Then some of the scribes and Pharisees said, "Master, we want to see a sign from you." But Jesus told them:

"It is an evil and unfaithful generation that craves for a sign, and no sign will be given to it—except the sign of the prophet Jonah." MATTHEW 12:38-39 (Phillips)

The Fifth Step:
John Lipscomb

"No sign will be given —"

I have pondered that verse a lot since so many signs
began to be given to us, signs of God's mighty power
at work in lives today. And I've discovered a deeper
truth in it than I first realized.

Of *course* no sign will be given to a faithless generation. How *can* it? How *can* a sign be given to an unfaithful, unbelieving generation — to those who are
unwilling to *receive* a sign?

Unbelievers have to have everything explained in
terms of known scientific laws. They refuse to acknowledge laws higher than the ones they can catalog
and understand. But to a faith-*full* generation? A believing generation? Why, for them, there are signs
everywhere!

John Lipscomb had certainly been given a sign, I
knew, as I read a newspaper account about him late in
1967. It sounded as if he must be a believer, all right,
because a mighty sign was given to him. Think of it?
He had been buried alive! I wanted to talk to him.

On New Year's Day, when my husband didn't have
to hold court, we set out with three of our children for
an hour's drive to Fuquay-Varina where John Lipscomb made his home. Unable to contact him by tele-

phone we had gone on faith that we would find him at home. Stopping for directions several times, we parked in front of his house just as he drove up into the yard. He'd been to Raleigh that morning, pumping water from a ditch.

I could tell from the pictures of Jesus on the walls of his modest but comfortable home that John was a man who had been acquainted with his Lord for some time. Faith was no brand new thing with him. It might have begun small as a grain of mustard seed but now it flourished like a mighty tree, able to shelter him from the storms of life.

As we talked that day, and as we saw the place where a sign happened to John Lipscomb, my faith in the awesome power and presence of God was magnified. Here is John's story as he told it to us that day.

"It was a Tuesday morning six days before Christmas when Wade McNeil and I went to Ed Scott's place to clean out his well. We backed up the truck and took the rocks and boards off the top so we could pump out the water. It didn't take long.

"When the water was out, Wade said he'd go down to catch the frogs. I never had liked frogs jumping around me in close places like that, and sometimes I let Wade go down to catch them. But I couldn't let him do it that day. I had the strangest feeling that if I let him go down he wouldn't come up alive.

"So I told Wade I'd catch the frogs myself. He could stay on top and operate the crane that lowers and raises the bucket. I put on my boots, raincoat and my hard hat. I took along my shovel to dig up the trash.

"Something still didn't seem just right to me, but I couldn't figure out what it was. So, I stopped on the rim of the well, just inside the curbing, and did what I usually do before going down into a well. I prayed, 'Lord, take care of me.' Then I stepped into the steel bucket hooked onto the end of the cable Wade was controlling and told him to let me down.

"The well is about 40 feet deep and probably five feet across, the walls shored up with big rocks. I caught the frogs, shoveled some dirt and trash and let Wade hoist the bucket to empty it. Then I leaned over to pry up what looked like a piece of junk sticking out near the bottom of the well. The piece of junk turned out to be the corner of a really big rock. As soon as I realized that, I stopped tugging — but it was too late.

"The noise was like a bad wreck — like cars smashing together. In a split second I looked up and saw the whole top of the well breaking loose and tearing up and throwing itself right down at me, blacking out the sky.

" 'Lord, help me!' I shouted. I threw up my right hand and pulled my hard hat down over my face.

"There wasn't anywhere I could run, so I just leaned into the wall, like I was leaning on Jesus.

"I had learned to lean on Him about twenty years ago. I wasn't a praying man then; I was kind of rough. And bad things kept happening to me. I had a lot of close calls. A train ran into a car I was riding in and cut off the front bumper. I was hurt when a car ran into a train. Then, another night, I was out walking along the high bank above the railroad track. It was wet and the red clay was slick. I lost my footing and fell all the way down to the bottom, onto the tracks. Bruised and dizzy, I suddenly sickened of my way of life. Right then I laid down the world and went to God. I'd carried Him with me every place I'd gone since. He'd been good to lean on, lots of times.

"I kept leaning on Him, while the rocks and dirt rained down beside me — an awful rumbling and thundering. They kept coming, filling up the well as high as my head, and kept on falling. The whole time I

45

prayed, 'God, take care of me.' And big boulders miraculously missed me; the smaller stuff just bounced off my hard hat.

"When the rocks finally stopped, everything got still. I couldn't move — I was pinned against the wall. I couldn't see — it was dark as night. I was buried alive. So I just kept on leaning and praying.

"After a minute I heard feet running. I knew Wade was going for help. I remembered that Ed Scott had already gone to work. Wade would have to run clear down the hill, through the cornfield and across the highway to Forney's store to find any men to help him.

"There wasn't much air in the little breathing pocket my hat made. And what there was seemed almost too dusty to breathe. I couldn't get scared. I knew that. I was short of breath already and had to keep breathing slow and easy. 'Lord, help me,' I prayed and He did. My breathing levelled off and was easier.

"Time passed. How long? Maybe 10 . . . 20 . . . 30 minutes. Then far off I heard voices, '. . . bound to be dead by now . . . the well's half filled.'

"I shouted loud as I could. 'Alive . . . alive.' But my voice was muffled. Could they hear?

"Then I felt rocks being moved above me. How long would it take? I was beginning to choke and gasp from lack of air. 'Breathe slowly and don't panic. Breathe slowly . . .'

"I knew Wade was up above, and I figured Merlin Prince and Garland Forney and Ben McCoy were there too. They would get me out. But I needed air. I kept praying and leaning and telling myself to 'b-r-e-a-t-h-e s-l-o-w-l-y.'

"Then suddenly there was fresh air! I gulped it in, gratefully. A rescue truck had arrived and oxygen was being pumped to me by a hose through the rocks and dirt.

46

"Hours later my rescuers got down close to my head. Since there was room for but one man to work, it was Merlin Prince who removed a 50 pound rock above my head and worked his torn and bleeding hands down to get the smaller rocks away from around my face.

"Finally my head was free! I could look up and see out. The day was cloudy, but I'd never seen a brighter sky!

"A little after four o'clock, I was pulled up to the top. I had been buried alive for nearly six hours by 15 feet of fallen rock, nine of it over my head.

"The doctors examined me at the hospital but they couldn't find a thing wrong — not even a bruise — so they let me go home.

"Lots of folks have been coming to see us since the well caved in. At first they say I'm lucky to be alive. But when they look at that tremendous pile of rocks that covered me, they know it wasn't luck that saved me, it was leaning on Jesus."

Don't allow yourself to be overpowered by evil. Take the offensive — overpower evil with good! ROMANS 12:21 (Phillips)

Forgive, I pray you, the transgression of your brothers and their sin, because they did evil to you. GENESIS 50:17 (RSV)

Then Peter came to Jesus and asked, "Lord, how many times can my brother sin against me and I have to forgive him? Seven times?" "No, not seven times," answered Jesus, "but seventy times seven." MATTHEW 18:21-22 (TEV)

The Sixth Step:
Hostage

More than a year after we'd visited John Lipscomb, I
read a newspaper account about Ruth and Isley Wilcox, two people who were praising God for deliverance, when it looked to me as if they hadn't been
delivered at all. We went to see them a few weeks later
and learned something about forgiveness.

It all began early one morning in the summer of
1969 —

"We interrupt this program to bring you a special
news bulletin. Two convicts have just escaped from
the Robeson County Prison Camp. They are armed —
and dangerous. They have killed one guard and taken
another hostage. Ricardo Resendez, 26, a Mexican-
American, is short, with dark hair and a swarthy com-
plexion. Jimmy Lee, 21 —"

The announcer went on, but Ruth and Isley Wilcox
didn't hear him. They hadn't turned the radio on that
morning or the TV. They'd had no warning that this
would be the most terrifying day of their lives.

Both were sitting on the back porch of their comfortable brick home, preparing snap beans for the
freezer. Ruth had picked the beans after hanging her
Monday wash on the line. Isley had been crating eggs
and seeing to other details of running his farms. Nei-

ther had any premonition about the two pairs of eyes that watched their every move from the edge of the pine trees at the back of the yard.

When the beans were finished, Isley stood up and stretched. At sixty-seven he was tall and erect, vigorous looking. "Think I'll go back to lie down and rest my eyes," he said. Ruth nodded. Isley needed his rest. She would be glad when he could have the operation to remove the cataracts that blurred his vision. The doctor had said it would be just a few more weeks.

Ruth picked up the pan of beans and went through the screen door into the kitchen. A quick dark shape in the woods melted closer to the house, finding ready concealment behind the tall pines and neat outbuildings.

Standing at the sink, Ruth smiled when she heard a noise on the porch. Their nine cats were forever tipping chairs over and causing brooms and mops to clatter to the floor.

The clock said 11:25, time to be getting dinner under way so it would be ready when Isley's 16 year old son, Lynn, came to the house. Teenagers had bottomless pits for stomachs. Having raised a family of her own, Ruth knew how to fill them up. She and Isley had both lost their first mates. They'd married each other just eighteen months ago, ending years of loneliness.

Ruth turned away from the counter to go to the refrigerator, but stopped abruptly. A man stood just inside the door, close enough for her to touch.

"Lady, is your husband at home?" The man seemed nervous, in a hurry.

Strangers came to see Isley all the time. Ruth wasn't surprised that she'd never seen this one before. He was short, for a man, and dark. His clothing didn't fit him very well — some kind of uniform, gray, with a

52

stripe down the side, the shirt so big it was all knotted up at the waist. A too-big cap was pushed back on his dark hair.

"Yes, he's here," she said, recovered from being momentarily startled. "Just have a seat and I'll go get him." She gestured toward a kitchen chair and headed for the den. But the man didn't sit down, he stayed close behind her. Maybe he hadn't heard.

"Just have a seat," she said again, without turning around. She motioned toward a couch in the den this time. The man paid no attention. He walked so close behind her that she could feel him as she continued across the den and started down the long hallway toward Isley's bedroom. Something hard jabbed at the middle of her back. It gave her an eerie feeling.

She could see into the bedroom now. Isley wasn't asleep.

"Honey," she called, "there's someone here to see you." She stood aside so the man could go into the room. But he stayed behind her, waiting.

Isley sat up, turned, and put his feet on the floor. He strode across the room to the hallway. He saw the man standing behind Ruth.

The man stepped out and stuck a .38 in his face. "Back up!" he spat out.

Ruth gasped and flung a hand to her throat. What did it mean?

"I don't want no trouble — git to the kitchen!" The words were staccato, menacing.

Isley Wilcox began to pray.

His belief in prayer was no puny, intellectual thing. Years ago he had learned the practicality of prayer, the awesome power of it. When, in 1949, accountants had found a mistake in bookkeeping that meant he owed over thirty thousand dollars in back taxes, he was greatly dismayed and overwhelmingly burdened. How could he ever pay it all?"

He had taken that problem to the Lord, getting on his knees in an old pack house on the farm, one of several secret places where he often confronted his God. When he left the building, still not knowing how he could pay what was owed, but trusting that the Lord would show him the way, he felt as if a great weight had been lifted from his back.

And, mysteriously, without any other explanation than the grace of God at work, Isley's farms prospered, enabling him to pay off his tax debt in three years. The farms had never done so well, before or since.

Now Isley was praying for his life, and that of his wife, as they were prodded down the hall at gunpoint. The man indicated they were to sit in chairs at the kitchen table. Keeping his gun trained on them, he stepped to the door and motioned to someone outside. Through the window at the end of the table Isley saw a man sneak furtively from behind the smokehouse up to the back door. He was armed, too, and stood at the other end of the room, not taking his eyes from Isley or Ruth for a second.

"We just broke jail," the first man barked. "We got the gas chamber starin' us in the face fer killin' a guard so we got nuthin' to lose. One or two more lives won't make no difference to us." His gun was cocked as he talked and paced the floor. He swung it back and forth, gesticulating wildly.

"We aim to wait here 'til the law cools off and then make our getaway later, when they think we're already gone, see? And yer gonna help us. We won't hurt ya — *if* ya do 'zactly like I tell ya. Unnerstand? We don't want no trouble."

"You won't have any trouble," Isley assured him. "We don't want trouble either. We're Christians, and we try to live it."

Ruth Wilcox felt herself swaying in her chair. "I'm

getting faint," she whispered. "There's some ammonia there in the cupboard. Could I —"

Resendez opened the door to which she pointed and poured some ammonia into a glass. She filled it with water, drank it and sat back down. Resendez's gun followed her every move.

The two convicts held a whispered conference at the end of the room, keeping out of range of the windows. Their eyes — and their guns — stayed on Ruth and Isley, who were not permitted to talk to each other.

"You expectin' anyone today?" Resendez wanted to know.

Ruth nodded. "Isley's son, Lynn, for dinner at one o'clock," she said.

Resendez thought for a moment. "We can handle the boy," he decided, swinging his gun again.

Then he turned the radio on. The news was full of the escape. Police had found the second guard, tied up in a car hidden in some underbrush just a mile from the Wilcox home. Bloodhounds were being brought to trail the escapees. Law enforcement officers were summoned from miles around.

Ruth wondered how long they would take — and whether the dogs would track the convicts to her house. She felt nauseated and needed to use the bathroom. Would they let her?

Resendez nodded his assent, and, still brandishing the gun, indicated that she could use the half-bath adjoining the kitchen. As she entered the tiny room she saw Resendez's hat — the guard's hat — lying on the floor in the corner where he had flung it. Her heart bounded. She could throw the hat out the window onto the front lawn where someone might see it — She reached for the door, to close it behind her.

Resendez stuck his foot out. "The door stays open," he sneered. He stood in the hallway, watching, until

Ruth was ready to go back into the kitchen. The hat lay untouched on the floor.

A car crunched into the drive. There were footsteps to the front door. The doorbell rang insistently. Resendez made Ruth answer it, while he stood behind the door with his gun trained on her. She knew Isley was in the sights of Lee's gun and that Lee was under orders to shoot at the first sign or sound of anything out of the way. Ruth tried to act natural as she opened the door.

The Chief of Police stood on the top step. He was just checking to make sure they were all right, he said. He told her about the escaped prisoners. Wanting desperately to tell him that the convicts were in her house, but afraid of endangering her husband, Ruth spoke reassuring words. But she winked her left eye and risked a barely perceptible pointing gesture with her hand. The Chief didn't see it, but turned his back and walked away.

When Lynn came home, Resendez told him, "Stay in the yard. Look normal." Then he pushed his revolver against Isley's temple. "If you want to see your old man alive when this day is over, don't try *anything.* No warnings, no nuthin'. Is that clear?" Resendez's manner spoke louder than words. Lynn nodded and swallowed. He would be obedient. They all would.

The phone rang.

"Answer it — and act natural," Resendez commanded. He went to the phone with Ruth, holding a gun to her head as he leaned close to hear both sides of the conversation.

"Are you all right?" Ruth's sister-in-law asked.

"Oh, yes, we're fine," Ruth lied, watching Lee with his gun trained on Isley's head.

"Well, we were just wondering — with the prison break and all. Be sure to keep your doors locked.

Those two are bad ones, from what I hear."

Ruth was about to find out how bad they were.

Resendez let Lee stand guard over Ruth and Isley for a few minutes while he went to a bedroom to change his clothes, putting on some that belonged to Lynn. He brought out an extra pair of khaki pants and took Ruth and Isley to the living room, at the back of the house. Lynn had gone outside, convinced that his father's life depended upon his being perfectly obedient.

Resendez cut the khaki pants into long strips with a sharp knife. Then he ordered Isley to lie face down on the floor of the carpeted living room. He bound his hands tightly behind him, and tied his feet and legs together. It seemed unnecessary. Isley hadn't been any trouble to them. He'd made no effort to escape, or to betray them, just had sat quietly, praying silently.

But the convicts were making sure he wouldn't try anything while they took care of their business with his wife. Resendez was first, leaving Lee on guard while he forced Ruth back to the bedroom. She cried, she pleaded with him, she reminded him about his own mother — all to no avail. He bound and gagged her. Then he had his way with her. Next, it was Lee's turn.

Later Lee cut the cloth that bound Isley and took him back to the bedroom, to keep him there at gunpoint.

Would the day ever end? Silent prayers filled the air. "Good Lord, deliver us, save us, help us. Glorify Thy Name."

People came to the door. Sometimes Ruth answered it, sometimes Lynn, after he came back in the house. "Isley's resting," Ruth said. "Come back tomorrow." Resendez, standing behind the door, kept the gun on her, told her what to say.

57

Twice during the interminable afternoon Ruth was put to bed with Isley. Lynn answered the door then, explaining that his father and stepmother were resting. Lee, guarding Mr. and Mrs. Wilcox, warned them from time to time that they'd better do everything Resendez told them, or — He seemed just as terrified of Resendez as they were.

Isley's son, George, came over three or four times that day, just to make sure his father was safe. Ruth told him that Isley was sleeping off a sleeping pill. He'd been having some trouble with his nerves and occasionally took sedatives.

When Ruth's daughter telephoned that she and her family were coming over later that evening, Ruth tried to talk her out of it. "Why don't you come tomorrow?" she said. She didn't want her teen-age granddaughters in that house. Not now. But Resendez insisted that she let them come. He didn't want anything to look suspicious, he said.

Once, when a daughter-in-law came to speak to Isley, she was permitted to go down the hallway to the bedroom. The poodle in her arms knew something was wrong, and he did his best to warn her, sniffing the air and looking in the direction of the bathroom that adjoined the bedroom. The bathroom door was standing halfway open. Lee was behind it — but the visitor didn't see him.

A dark cloud came up in the middle of the hot afternoon. Ruth saw it, and remembered her clothes on the line. Ordinarily she'd have brought them in long before now.

Resendez noticed the cloud too. He spent a lot of time looking out the windows, being careful not to be seen. He was surprised at the number of police cars cruising up and down. Would the activity ever subside so he and Lee could make their getaway? Someone was waiting for them in Fayetteville —

"You want the boy to bring the clothes in?" Resendez asked.

Ruth thought for a minute, not remotely aware that her decision would be an important one. "I guess not," she said. "It mightn't be safe. The lightning could come down and run along the wire." Resendez nodded. He didn't know it would matter to him. He certainly didn't want any emergencies now. Neither he nor Ruth suspected that the clothes on the line were part of an answer to prayer.

And so the dry laundry flapped wildly in the wind until the rain came, leaving the clothes hanging heavy, sagging and dripping, some of them dragging the ground.

The law enforcement officers patrolling took note of the clothes on the line. They hung ghostly in the dark. Mrs. Wilcox wasn't the kind to leave her clean laundry out like that. But people had been going in and out all day. Surely there couldn't be anything wrong there. Or could there?

Something else seemed strange from the outside. There were four vehicles parked in the drive and not one had moved all afternoon — not the pickup truck nor any of the cars.

One patrolman, suspicious because of the clothes and the cars, turned into the drive that circled around behind the Wilcox house. Suddenly an outside light flashed on and off, three times! To the patrolman it looked like a signal, an S O S! Resendez's hand had flashed the light, accidentally, when he'd gone into the kitchen to watch the patrol car. He'd wanted to turn on a light — and had hit the wrong switch by mistake, three times, in quick succession. No one else in the house could have done that and lived. Resendez wasn't usually so clumsy. Was another Hand guiding his?

59

"Good Lord, save us, spare our lives." Ruth had prayed all day, as Isley had, putting his whole trust in Him. They'd walked a thin line of obedience, wanting to see tomorrow together when it dawned.

They had tried to witness to Resendez when he let them talk. "Jesus loves you, the Son of God died for your sins," they said. "He can make you clean again, make you new."

Resendez had jeered. "Can't nobody make me clean again," he boasted. "I'm too far in it now. I got no God."

"He forgives us, as we forgive others," Ruth heard herself say. In her heart she wondered, "But can I forgive them?" And she knew she must.

Ruth's daughter and her family came and sat down in the den. Isley was still "resting" back in the bedroom. Resendez guarded him now, while Lee kept vigil over Ruth and her callers from the front hallway. The convicts had moved a heavy dresser across the bedroom doorway as a barricade, just in case anyone should try to come in.

The clothes on the line, the cars in the yard, the suddenly flashing lights — It was just a hunch, a hunch that looked ridiculous in the light of all the day's visitors to the house, but the police decided to move in.

Meanwhile Ruth started to the front door with her daughter and her family, who were ready to leave. To her great surprise the ever-present shadow behind the front door was gone! Lee must have joined Isley and Resendez in the bedroom! Or was he still watching her from the darkened living room across the hall?

Ruth didn't dare say anything yet. And suddenly she didn't have to say a word. A police officer was on the front steps. "Get in a car, get under a car, get anywhere out of range — quickly," he said. Ruth and

Lynn needed no urging. They climbed into Ruth's daughter's car. Isley was in the house alone. Alone with Resendez and Lee.

The Wilcox yard was full of cars, now, cars with official insignia on the sides. More than two hundred law enforcement officers had converged on the area. The house was illuminated by brilliant floodlights from all directions.

And so the long night began. Isley was forced to remain in bed, not knowing whether his family was safe or not. Several times the convicts got him up to use him as a shield at the window, where they attempted to bargain with police officers. Several times Resendez stormed out with loud cursing over the telephone, as he talked to officers who had tapped into the line. His fiery temper stayed at the kindling point.

Houses in the community stayed open all night — for prayer. A telephone prayer chain was organized to ask all believers to pray for Isley Wilcox, that his life might be spared.

At three o'clock that morning, Isley found his faith at low ebb. Faith was all he had left, and he could feel it draining out of him. Resendez was still debating about which of three alternatives to choose. He could shoot it out, or kill himself, or surrender. Isley felt that all of the alternatives except the last one would begin with his own death.

He began to pray as he had never prayed before. He prayed for his family first. And then he prayed for faith in the power and love of God. He remembered Daniel saved in the lions' den, the Hebrew children brought to the promised land, Paul and Silas, miraculously delivered from prison. And he prayed for deliverance for himself.

As he prayed he felt himself filled with the peace that passes all understanding. He had such an assurance that their lives would be spared that he had to fight to keep from going to sleep — even while Resendez was still storming at the officers.

In less than twenty minutes Resendez and Lee were crouched at the foot of his bed, making plans for surrender.

Lee walked out a little after three in the morning. And strangely, the violent Ricardo Resendez let him do it.

Three and a half hours later, Resendez let an unarmed Major Garrison come into the Wilcox home, with his hands stretched high above his head. Resendez handed him his gun.

"Come on, Ricky," the Major said. And he walked docilely toward the patrol car. Isley Wilcox followed them out, praising the Lord for what He had done.

"Oh, I know some very bad things happened," he admits, looking sympathetically toward his wife.

Ruth nodded, hearing him tell it.

"We're not spared from certain bad experiences in this life," she said softly, "but what's important is what these experiences do to us. Isley and I have turned it all over to the Lord." There was no trace of bitterness in her look or in his. "He has helped us forgive those two men."

Isley agreed as he took Ruth's hand. "And He does it by filling us with Himself. Then we can not only forgive the men, we can pray for them, too."

Ruth and Isley had been glad to witness about their terrible day — not to gain sympathy for themselves — but in order that God might be glorified. After one day with the Wilcox family I began to understand forgiveness in a deeper way than I had seen it before. Their own account of their terrible experience came through low-key, almost matter-of-fact. It was because they had so completely forgiven, that the terror itself, the ugliness, had been taken away — almost as if it had never been.

I began to see that there was more power in forgiveness than I had ever dreamed.

Jesus then left the neighborhood of Tyre and went on through Sidon to Lake Galilee, going by way of the territory of the Ten Towns. Some people brought him a man who was deaf and could hardly speak, and begged Jesus to place his hand on him. So Jesus took him off alone, away from the crowd, put his fingers in the man's ears, spat, and touched the man's tongue. Then Jesus looked up to heaven, gave a deep groan, and said to the man, Ephphatha, *which means,* "Open up!" *At once the man's ears were opened, his tongue was set loose, and he began to talk without any trouble. Then Jesus ordered them all not to speak of it to anyone; but the more he ordered them, the more they told it. And all who heard were completely amazed.* "How well he does everything!" *they exclaimed.* "He even makes the deaf to hear and the dumb to speak!"* MARK 7:31-37 (TEV)

The Seventh Step:
Maria

It was one of the most important days of my life, but I
had no inkling of it as I relaxed after dinner with
friends. The men were still in the dining room, enjoy-
ing another piece of coconut cake. The children, five
of them mine, had scattered to ping-pong tables and
swings. We women were just talking, not about anything important.

Then one of them, a social worker, turned to me.
"Oh, by the way, Irene," she began, "maybe you can
advise me about a baby we've been trying to place for
adoption." Her manner and tone of voice were casual,
matter-of-fact.

But *something* made me sit up straight in my chair,
eagerly attentive. I felt an almost electrical awareness, a prickling sensation that began at the tips of my
toes and travelled to the top of my head. I didn't know
what was about to be said, but I knew that God had
some special purpose in it for me. I listened with every
nerve.

"It's strange," the social worker said. "Ordinarily
we'd have placed this baby long before now. She's
three and a half months old already and we've been
trying to find adoptive parents to match her coloring.
She's rather dark — her father was Italian."

"Did you find parents for her?" I interrupted. I didn't know any dark-skinned couple who wanted a baby but perhaps I could find one.

"We thought we had two weeks ago," she answered. "But when the prospective father examined the baby, he thought she couldn't hear. And he wanted a healthy, normal child. A pediatrician agreed that there was definitely *something* the matter with the baby. And, later, an audiologist tested her and found that she *is* severely hard-of-hearing."

So that was it! A dark-skinned hard-of-hearing baby who needed a home.

I hardly heard the social worker as she continued, explaining that she wanted the name and address of the correspondence school I'd used in teaching our three-year-old child who was profoundly deaf for the first year of her life.

"We won't be able to find adoptive parents for this baby now," the social worker went on. "We'll just have to keep her in foster homes until she's old enough to be sent away to the School for the Deaf. But maybe one of our foster mothers can help her a little before she's old enough for school."

Even as I sit here typing this, a year after that day, my arms sprout gooseflesh. There is still the electric Awareness, the certainty from Him, "Irene, this child is for you."

I didn't argue, but I imagine I swallowed audibly. Another baby for us? I was past forty and found my time fully occupied with the family I already had. But the Awareness didn't go away. Under my breath I murmured an assenting "Yes, Lord."

After a few moments I excused myself to go into the other room to speak to my husband, to tell him about the hard-of-hearing dark-skinned baby and about the Awareness. He felt it too and we returned to the living room together.

"You don't need the address of the correspondence school," I said. "We want to adopt the baby. Do you think we can have her?"

The social worker stared at me. "Why, I don't know —" she stammered. "You haven't even *seen* her. And with five other children already, what would you do with another one? Another handicapped one at that?"

"We don't know either, but we're *supposed* to take this one," my husband assured her. "Among other things she *needs* a noisy household and we can provide that."

We also knew how to work at teaching deaf babies. And there was a fine new State School for the Deaf just five minutes from our front door.

There was something else, too. Beginning that day we began to pray for the child, and asked our believing friends to pray that God's perfect will might be accomplished in her life.

Ten days later we saw the baby for the first time, not knowing yet whether we would be allowed to have her. Then, on Thursday morning, the telephone rang. "If you haven't changed your mind," the social worker said, "you may come to get your baby today." *Our baby* —

On the following Sunday, two weeks after we had first heard about her, my husband and I stood at the front of our church for the Mother's Day service of the blessing of babies. I held a curly-haired, dark-eyed, Maria in my arms. Our other children had named her, agreeing, "If no one else wants her it would be a shame for us not to take her."

We never doubted that we were doing the right thing. Our church and neighborhood had warmly accepted our own hard-of-hearing child. They would accept Maria too.

That normal children cost money to raise, that they

require time and patience and energy and love, we knew. We knew too that handicapped children require more of everything. In a way it didn't make sense for us to adopt a handicapped child — we already had our hands full with 'Guerite — but we didn't have to think about whether it made sense or not. God had said, "This child is for you." He hadn't asked, "Will you take her?"

So there was nothing to worry about. We thought God had given us a job to do and we trusted that He was able to provide the means. Looking back we could see already that Maria was the answer to two of our questioning prayers.

We had prayerfully considered whether we should have another child for our three-year-old 'Guerite to grow up with. She needed someone because our four older children were teens or almost teens already.

We had prayed too to know how we could thank Him for the healing He had worked in 'Guerite. Once "profoundly deaf" she had improved dramatically to where she was not merely "severely-hard-of-hearing." And she was even learning to talk! And so we decided that taking Maria for our own was one way of thanking God for blessings we had received from His hand.

We hadn't yet realized that Maria was His answer to a third prayer as well. But we were soon to find out.

Maria had blessed our home with her beautiful baby presence for three months when we kept the appointment with the audiologist for a check-up for both our babies. 'Guerite's marvelously improved but still imperfect hearing tested in the severely hard-of-hearing range, about the same as before.

And Maria? She sat on my lap as the audiologist called her name softly through one speaker facing us and then another in the opposite corner. Maria was like a spectator at a tennis match, turning her head first one way and then another as the source of the sound changed. There were other tests, all confirming what we had discovered and rejoiced about — Maria's hearing had become *perfectly* normal!

How often I had prayed, "Lord, help me with 'Guerite," as day by day I worked with her, trying to build speech where once there had been just the "unh, unh, unh" of a child who could not hear or understand. Maria was a perfect answer to that prayer. For what could help 'Guerite more than a normal, jabbering baby sister whose presence would be a constant stimulus to her language development?

Our friends have asked and we have wondered, "Was Maria really hard-of-hearing and God healed her after people began to pray for her? And after we accepted her — handicap and all? Or was there a wrong diagnosis in the beginning?"

Only God knows the answer to that but we know we would never have *heard* of Maria, much less been given her for our own, if she had not been thought to have a serious handicap. Maria is the answer He has provided to many of our prayers, and, by His grace, He got us to accept her.

I realize now that I misinterpreted what God said to me on that very special day. When I felt His, "Irene, this child is for you," I said "Yes, Lord," thinking he was giving me a *job* to do for Him.

But His words were not the words God would use to give someone a job. They were words to accompany the presentation of a gift! Maria is His very precious gift to us.

And I wonder if it isn't always so, that when we set out to be obedient to what we think God wants us to do for Him, we are always blessed far more abundantly than we could ask or think.

We have learned in this experience, as we have in so

71

many others, how hard it is to serve the Lord. Whenever we attempt to serve Him and the needs of His children, we find Him serving us and all our needs instead.

But to keep me from being puffed up with pride because of the wonderful things I saw, I was given a painful physical ailment, which acts as the Devil's messenger to beat me and keep me from being proud. Three times I prayed to the Lord about this, and asked him to take it away. His answer was, "My grace is all you need; for my power is strongest when you are weak." I am most happy, then, to be proud of any weaknesses, in order to feel the protection of Christ's power over me. I am content with weaknesses, insults, hardships, persecutions, and difficulties for Christ's sake. For when I am weak, then I am strong. II CORINTHIANS 12:7-10 (TEV)

The Eighth Step;
Cloudy and Clear

There was something special about Marjorie Hatton. I
sensed it when I met her. Her face radiated quiet joy,
the reflection of an inner light, as if she had had some
extraordinary experience. Would she share it with us?
I hoped so.

My husband and I, and our four older children were
attending an International Prayer Fellowship Conference. Marjorie and Bob Hatton were there too. Our
schedules were pretty well filled with prayer meetings
and songfests and speeches but there were *some* inter-
vals for getting acquainted with each other. Marjorie
and I were strangers at the beginning — but not for
long.

"A present Christ is an *active* Christ," a minister
friend of mine affirms. And what Marjorie Hatton
shared with me is a remarkable illustration of the
truth of it. Here is her story of the unforgettable day
when she and her husband knew the reality of the
presence of God.

"Margie?"

Still half asleep I murmured an uncomprehending
"Huh?" and burrowed back into my pillow. Then I
felt my husband touch my arm, his voice quavering as
he spoke again.

"Margie—I don't feel very well."

Bob's hand was icy, his voice pitifully weak. The realization shocked me full awake. I sat up and peered at him where he lay beside me.

"Bob, it's not —" I protested, but I knew heart attack symptoms too well by now to deny what was happening. He nodded feebly, his face ashen, and grimaced as he clutched his left arm in a futile effort to ease the pain.

I ran to the telephone and called the doctor and our son, Roger. Then, cautioning Bob not to move, I dressed as quickly as I could. His two previous heart attacks had made me familiar with the symptoms, but could not allay my apprehensions about this one.

The doctor arrived within ten minutes, took Bob's blood pressure, listened to his heart, and summoned an ambulance.

"I'll meet you at the hospital—we'll be ready for him," he said tersely.

The two ambulance attendants surveyed the narrow hallway from the living room to our bedroom and decided that a turn would be difficult to negotiate with the ambulance cot. So they left it in the living room and carried Bob to it, trying to joke with him about how they were going to take him for a ride. But one attendant began to administer oxygen as soon as they got Bob into the ambulance, and the joking stopped. I rode beside Bob, my heart in my mouth, and our son followed in his car.

Bob was taken immediately to a second floor room and lifted gently into a bed. I stood at the foot of it while nurses gave hypodermics and the doctor and his assistants hooked Bob up to the electrocardiograph apparatus. They continued to administer oxygen while I tried to reassure Bob and keep him from the over-exertion of too much talking.

76

My reassuring words must have sounded phony. I needed reassurance myself. Bob's heart had been severely damaged by previous attacks, and his heart was greatly enlarged. I knew the heart machine had a telephone connection to a heart specialist in West Palm Beach, 45 miles east of Pahokee, but I hoped Bob's condition wasn't so critical as to require the specialist's help.

Bob's voice seemed a little stronger as he told me several things he wanted me to do for him. They were inconsequential to me—business affairs that could be attended to another day, but I knew Bob wouldn't relax fully until they were accomplished. Like most heart patients, Bob found keeping his affairs in order quite essential to his peace of mind. I had learned *that* from experience too.

Knowing the importance of sparing him any avoidable anxiety, I reluctantly left him in the doctor's hands and let Roger drive me to our house. There I got Bob's Bible, his pajamas, his razor and the electric toothbrush he wanted to have.

When I left the house in my car, I noticed that the gas gauge registered empty. Hating to be away from Bob even a minute longer than I had to, I just trusted there would be enough gas to get me back to the hospital. I bought documentary stamps for some legal papers and took them to our auditor as Bob had asked me to do. And I paid several bills he was concerned about. I did make one extra stop—at our church, to ask the secretary to be in prayer for Bob and to notify our prayer group of his desperate need for their prayers. But I wasn't really aware of how desperate the need was, at that moment.

Relieved to have completed all these matters in a relatively short time, I drove back to the hospital, arriving just in time to see an ambulance on its way out of the driveway.

77

"Bob is in that ambulance," a voice inside me warned. For an instant I was tempted to turn and follow it, but my saner judgment reminded me of the reading on my gas gauge and suggested that I ought to see the doctor first, to make sure that Bob was in the ambulance.

Inside the hospital I went to the second floor where Bob had been. A sea of sad faces—Bob's doctor and the nurses—confronted me.

Dr. Poteete, who is a close friend of ours, shook his head when he saw me.

"Margie," he said, "Bob is in critical condition, and there was *nothing* I could do for him. I've sent him to West Palm Beach where they have better facilities—"

The whole world fell out from under me.

"Oh, why did you have to send him?" I asked despairingly. "Won't the trip be too much—?"

Dr. Poteete explained that Bob was already in heart failure, that his lungs were rapidly filling up with fluid, and that he was spitting blood.

"These are the signs of the end of life," he said simply, and as gently as he could. Then he continued, his voice full of sympathy, "There's not a ghost of a chance, Margie." He spread his hands, their palms upward in a gesture of eloquent hopelessness. "Bob is dying—but I felt I had to let the heart specialist *try*. There wasn't time to wait for you to come back," he apologized.

I nodded, forgiving him. Something urged me to start for West Palm Beach immediately. The doctor thought I should not go alone, but wait for Roger, or Bob's brother and his son, Joe, who is a doctor.

It was sound advice, and I got on the elevator, full of discouragement. It seemed so important for me to be on my way. Reaching the first floor, I was headed for the exit when understanding flooded over me, and I exclaimed aloud.

78

"Why, I won't have to wait for any of them! I can go myself—because I'm not alone! Jesus is with me! He'll go!"

If anyone heard me talking to myself as I hurried down the corridor, they paid no attention.

Turning into the first gas station, I asked the attendant to give me enough gas to get me to the hospital in West Palm Beach. I couldn't afford to wait for any more. Briefly explaining the urgent circumstances, I was on my way without having to pay or to sign a ticket.

The road from Pahokee to West Palm Beach runs along a canal twenty feet deep. But I forgot about that hazard, concentrating on trying to catch up with the ambulance. I drove—fast—and prayed—hard. My life seemed spread out before me, especially the places where I hadn't done a good enough job.

When I noticed my speedometer registering 90 miles an hour, I saw that the car was getting too hot. I wouldn't be much help to Bob alongside the road in a burned-up car, so I slowed to about 70.

But it was too late. A State Highway Patrol cruiser loomed behind me, its light flashing insistently, before I could get down to a legal 60 miles per hour. *I couldn't stop for him!*

Rolling my window down, I shouted as he pulled alongside. "My husband is dying," I said.

"If *you* don't slow down, lady, *you'll* by dying too," he warned. But he turned his light off, dropped behind, and made a U turn back to where he came from.

"Thank you, Lord," I prayed, and stayed within the speed limit the rest of the way, telling God all the things in my heart. I asked my Heavenly Father to forgive me if there was anything I had ever done to hurt Bob. Then I began to give him to God. I actually lifted him into the Kingdom and asked God to receive him.

79

Bob was *such* a wonderful person—he truly loved his Lord, and he had been so loving and good to me.

Becoming calmer as I talked with Him, I made one last request, and then relinquished it.

"Lord, I would like to talk to Bob one more time, really I would, just to tell him I'm here, and that I love him. But, Lord, I give him to You *now*. You take him into Your Kingdom. Do what You know to be best."

Immediately I was filled with a strange peace—and tears of *joy* streamed down my face! I had never before felt so humble! Or so trusting!

And then I was aware of the cloud—a fluffy, wispy cloud, a cloud that belonged in the mountains. But it wasn't in the mountains, it wasn't even in the sky. It was right on the ground, completely enveloping my car! Although I could see its boundaries, I wasn't moving through it. It was travelling right along with me!

I strained my eyes to make sure they were not playing tricks on me. But there it was—extending about twenty feet in front of the car, thirty feet to the right and ten feet to the left. And, in the midst of it, I had an absolute sense of the very presence of God.

A voice, as loud and clear as my own, said to me, "Bob is full of the Holy Spirit."

Believing that Bob must have died, I answered, "Thank you, Lord, for taking him to be with You."

As suddenly as it had appeared, the cloud was gone, vanished from my sight.

I found myself stopped at a traffic light in West Palm Beach. Pulling up beside a Highway Patrolman who was directly in front of me, I asked if he could escort me to the hospital. He declined, but directed me to the shortest route, which I knew well from previous trips. I thanked him, and went on, still praising God.

There was a parking place right next to the hospital

80

entrance so I left my car and asked a "pink lady" to walk with me to the first floor, Dillman Wing, where heart patients were taken.

"My mind isn't really as clear as it should be," I told her.

We found Bob—very much alive and quite alert. He was giving the nurses instructions, as they moved him from the ambulance cot into a bed. That was Bob, always capable of getting a job done right!

"I watched for you out the back window all the way, Margie," Bob said. "I knew you'd get here. And the strangest thing happended to me on the way over—"

"Tell me later, Bob," I interrupted. I was too full to listen, or to talk. I knew there would be a "later" now. There was no need to hurry anymore.

About a month later I went to Dr. Poteete's office in Pahokee to make an appointment for Bob's check-up. He'd stayed in the hospital only three weeks where he was treated for pneumonia and a weak heart.

Dr. Poteete had something to tell me.

"You know, Margie," he confided, his face wearing a baffled expression, *"something* happened to Bob between here and West Palm Beach—because he was dying when he left—"

"I know," I said, but couldn't explain.

Bob knew it too. One day I let him tell me.

With a hint of mystery in his eyes, he said, "Something *did* happen to me on the way to West Palm Beach in the ambulance. I had a vivid awareness that God was right there with me, that I belonged to Him. I was actually able to talk to the Lord and ask Him to take care of me. And I wasn't afraid to die—"

I nodded, because I knew the mystery too. I had been in the midst of the Cloud that made everything clear, especially the very real presence of God and an ever-growing experience of Christ in our lives.

81

Oh, there is still a heart problem—we live with that all the time. But it's not the center of our lives, God is.

When he came home from the hospital, Bob knew that God had a job for him to do, that He'd spared him for some special purpose. He didn't know exactly what, but thought it had something to do with prayer. And while he was waiting to know, he began to witness about his experience to others. Our brush with death had helped us know what life is really all about.

The first of this year Bob was used to begin three prayer groups in our church, groups that know they can expect great things to happen, through believing faith. They never know just *how* God will do it, but they do know He blesses each one who truly turns to Him in trust.

Bob is gradually retiring from his farming business, letting our sons take over. And he's rapidly moving—by leaps and bounds—into the new business revealed to him: showing others how God's strength is made perfect in our weakness.

Train up a child in the way he should go: and when he is old, he will not depart from it. PROVERBS 22:6 (KJV)

The Ninth Step:
Victoria Whitehead

If we are to follow the way everlasting, we have to let
faith apply to the very mundane, the most ordinary
events of our days, as well as to the spectacular ones.
Life has to become a very "practice of the presence of
God" all the time.

Recently I met a woman whose life exemplified this
important secret, which I had finally begun to grasp.

It had been a hectic day for me — as usual — with
more things to do than time to do them. But now I
needed to put all the frustrations out of my mind so I
could listen to the remarkable eighty-three-year-old
woman I had come to interview. Surprisingly, I could
almost feel the serenity that pervaded her neat brick
home settle on me as I entered the living room and sat
down.

Victoria Whitehead's bright blue eyes were twin-
kling, her hands quietly folded as she waited for my
questions. She had certainly earned her serenity, I
thought, after raising such a large and successful family. Twelve children! How had she done it! Losing two
in infancy she had seen eight of them through college.
Seven had their Master's degrees and an eighth was
working on hers. There'd been no automatic washers
to help her, no ready-to-eat food or ready-to-wear

clothes from the store, no permanent pressed fabrics.

My own six were a small family by comparison. Yet I stayed unbelievably busy. Would I too have earned serenity when they were grown?

Wondering at Victoria Whitehead's secret, I fumbled in my overburdened purse for a pencil and opened my notebook.

There a boldly printed message shouted at me.

"*Puh-leeze, Mama,*" it scolded, in a scrawl I recognized as belonging to my youngest son, "*don't forget to come home in time to take me to my piano lesson this time!*" Every word was underscored with heavy strokes.

I reddened, remembering how James had missed his last lesson because I had gone to a church meeting and failed to get home on time. Now I tucked the reminder out of sight, hoping no one had noticed it, and began asking questions.

Victoria was the oldest one of three children when her mother died. Because her grandparents were still busy raising large families of their own, she went to live with her great grandparents. It wasn't long before Victoria had to stop going to school in order to nurse her aging relatives. She decided then, that if she ever had children of her own, they would all go to school every day, for as long as she could possibly send them.

"I knew what it was to come up without going to school much," she said, shaking her head at the sadness of it.

"Education is important," I agreed, "especially these days. But how did you manage to do it all?"

"Oh, I didn't do it all by myself," she explained. "My husband was living then. He had a good job — making bricks and later working for an oil company — and all the children helped me a lot. Everyone had something to do. They chopped wood, picked vegetables from the garden, shelled the peas, fed the pigs, picked cotton in the fall, helped with the canning, straightened the house, swept the yard, and laid their clean clothes out at night for school the next day."

My own thoughts intruded. *Getting clothes out at night instead of as a last minute scramble in the morning could smooth the day at our house.* My conscience nudged harder. *Especially if I would get the ironing done when I should.*

Mrs. Whitehead continued to reminisce about the happy years. She didn't make them sound hectic at all. "The older ones helped the little ones with their homework," she said. "And, in the morning, one tended the baby while I started a fire and cooked the biscuits and bacon for breakfast. My husband had to go to work early, and the children carried his breakfast to him on their way to school."

I felt vaguely guilty. When my husband had to get an early start he helped himself to dry cereal in the kitchen or stopped for a bite uptown.

"Didn't someone tell me you used to do sewing for other people?" Thinking of the endless overflowing of the mending basket at my house I doubted that she had really had time to sew for others.

"Oh, yes," she beamed. "I always made all our clothes and sewed a lot for other people. Money was hard to come by, sometimes —" A faraway look came into her eyes. "There were depressions — but everyone always had to have someone make clothes for them. Many's the night I've stayed up all night to sew. I couldn't sew much in the daytime," she explained. "The children had to come first."

The children had to come first? Oh, but things were different then. I have so many other things to do — important things —

"*One thing is needful —*"

87

Now why did that bit of scripture have to pop into my head just now?

"Mostly," she smiled, "mostly we had good times. And when we had bad ones, like when all the children had whooping cough at the same time, I'd try not to complain. I'd just think, 'Well, it could be worse,' and we got along all right."

Mrs. Whitehead tilted her head at the sound of children shouting in the street outside, and gestured toward the front of the house. "Seems like nowadays too many children just go where they want to go," she said. "And their parents are working away from home, and so they don't know — or seem to care."

She sighed and paused for a moment. "I never let my children play in the street. There was a house, down a little way, and on the other side of the street. There were children there and my children loved to play with them — but they were never allowed to go without asking permission. When they'd ask, I'd say, 'Yes, you may go. But be home by five o'clock.'

"They'd go and play for a while and then ask Miss Gert, 'What time is it? Mama told us not to stay too long, and to be home by five o'clock.' And they'd always be back on time."

Oh, that would be wonderful! I thought of the hours I'd spent, and the energy I'd wasted, scouring the neighborhood for my own strays, when supper was on the table.

"Seems like parents today don't have as much time," Victoria surmised. "There are too many places for them to go." I nodded at that. "They don't take time to train their children, or to keep up with where they're going, and who they're with, and when they should be home. And they don't have time to read the Bible together like we did. They're on the go all the time."

88

I had to agree with that too. Hadn't our own nightly Bible reading with the children declined from grand beginning to a mere verse or two as we hurried away to outside activities? I was guilty, all right.

Mrs. Whitehead clucked a "tsk, tsk!" and her daughter, who had taken me to visit, laughed.

"Now, Mama," she chided, shaking her finger, "remember the favorite scripture you used to quote to us: 'Fret not thyself because of evildoers . . .'"

Evildoers? Why, that's what we are, isn't it? Parents who neglect their children and run off to tend to other people's business are evildoers — and I was one of them!

But I didn't mean to be! I thought about James and his piano lesson, looked at my watch, and saw there was still time for one more question — a big one.

"What do you think *really* made the difference?" I asked her. "Was it that you had more time? Was it that you had such dreams for your children? Or how is it that your big family turned out to be such helpers of mankind — teachers, nurses, speech therapists — when so many just don't make it?"

"What made the difference?" She repeated my question, thinking about it. And her eyes, their sight, and not their brilliance, dimmed with cataracts, grew misty with remembering. "What made the difference? The Lord did. God made the difference. You have to put Him out in front to start with. He'll look out for you if you put your trust in Him."

Victoria's daughter recalled the time, years ago, when her mother had been hospitalized with a serious kidney ailment. One kidney was removed, Victoria's weight fell to eighty-seven pounds and the doctors despaired of her recovery.

"We're going to try one more thing," they told her. "We're going to stop all medication — it doesn't seem

89

to be helping you anyway — and just send you home. We'll just leave you in the hands of the Lord."

The doctors had sounded discouraged. But not Victoria. She glowed with confidence and hope.

"You're going to leave me in the Lord's hands?" she exclaimed. "Oh, but that's *good!* I've been *there* all the time!"

Driving home, in time to take James to his piano lesson, I realized that serenity wasn't a thing Victoria had earned and come to in her old age when her children were grown and her life's work ended.

No, serenity had been her secret all along — because she had trained her children up in the way they should go, and she had put her trust in the Lord. He *had* looked after her.

It was a secret worth knowing — and applying more fruitfully in my own life.

But as for you, continue in the truths that you were taught and firmly believe. For you know who your teachers were, and you know that ever since you were a child you have known the Holy Scriptures, which are able to give you the wisdom that leads to salvation through faith in Christ Jesus. For all Scripture is inspired by God and is useful for teaching the truth, rebuking error, correcting faults, and giving instruction for right living, so that the man who serves God may be fully qualified and equipped to do every kind of good work. 2 TIMOTHY 3:14-17 (TEV)

A Landing:
Hearts and Powers

"All scripture is inspired by God —" But is it *really* relevant to today's living? After all, the world has changed *so* much since our Bible came into being. How could such ancient writings be thought to have current application?

I have encountered some sermons and read some books that seemed to indicate that we must somehow *make* the Bible relevant.

But, for some of us, *reading* the Bible is all that's required, not to *make* it relevant, but to discover its eternal relevancy, not merely to life in general, but to specific situations in which we need guidance.

One such specific situation, a *very* modern one, came to my attention recently. David DuPlessis, well known Pentecostal, described it as he spoke to a Full-Gospel meeting I attended.

It seems that the doctor who was to help Dr. Christiaan Barnard perform the first heart transplant had what he called a "conscientious problem." He wondered if God would be displeased if he changed men's hearts, from one body to another in order to prolong life.

After he and Dr. Barnard had prayed about the problem, seeking to know God's will in it, he began to search the scriptures to see what God had to say. Imagine! Searching the scriptures, the ancient Book, for advice about such a modern thing as heart transplants! It hardly made sense.

But the doctor found something — exactly what he needed — in Ezekiel 36:26 (KJV). There he read:

"A new heart also will I give you, and a new spirit will I put within you: and I will take away the stony heart out of your flesh, and I will give you an heart of flesh."

Talk about relevance!

"Why, this is transplant!" he said. "You take out one heart — you put in another heart. That's a transplant! And if my heavenly Father considers this principle in order, to exchange hearts, then I think we can do it too."

History records that they did — and the operation was a successful one.

Frequently, even "happened upon" scriptures speak to a concern of our hearts. We have all heard of people who pray and then, opening their Bibles at random for guidance, are met by a text that is of immense benefit to them. I've had the same thing happen to me on more than one occasion.

Once, sitting in the little International Prayer Room at Lake Junaluska, preparing myself for a talk I was to make that day before the International Prayer Fellowship Conference, I prayed for a scripture to use in my preliminary remarks. The passage that greeted my eyes as I let my *Good News for Modern Man* (the very helpful American Bible Society translation of the New Testament) fall open was exactly right:

"I give thanks to Christ Jesus our Lord, who has given me strength for my work. I thank him for considering me worthy, and appointing me to serve him, even though in the past I spoke evil of him, and persecuted and insulted him. But God was merciful to me, because I did not believe and so did not know what I was doing. And our Lord poured out his abundant grace on me and gave me the faith and love which are ours in union with Christ Jesus. This is a true saying, to be completely accepted and believed: Christ Jesus came into the world to save sinners. I am the worst of them, but it was for this very reason that God was merciful to me, in order that Christ Jesus might show his full patience with me, the worst of sinners, as an example for all those who would later believe in him and receive eternal life. To the eternal King, immortal and invisible, the only God — to him be honor and glory for ever and ever! Amen." I Timothy 1:12-17 (TEV)

Appropriate? It was Thanksgiving Day (the passage was entitled "Gratitude for God's Mercy") and my talk was a personal witness about my strayings from the Lord and how He had brought me back!

More recently I was in prayer for a precious young man who was, very unexpectedly, found to have lung cancer. On the eve of his scheduled surgery we had talked to him at length on the telephone. And he, who had grown up denying God, was now more than ready to use the rest of his life thanking and praising and serving His newly acknowledged Saviour. He was still apprehensive about the surgery, however, and, on the morning when it was to be performed, I found myself longing for some appropriate faith-strengthening scriptural meditation for the day.

As I stood at the counter in my kitchen, folding clean clothes from the dryer, my eye fell on an open Moffatt Bible displayed there on a bookholder a friend had given me for Christmas. There to greet me were beautiful words I'd never discovered before:

"My soul is bowed to the dust: revive me, even as thou
   hast promised;
   teach me thine orders, thou who answerest me when
I tell thee of my plight;
   show me how thy will works, that I may muse upon
thy wondrous deeds.
My soul is melting under trouble: nerve me, as thou
hast promised;
   keep me from being false to thee, and graciously
direct me.
A faithful life is what I choose, thy demands are my
desire;
   O thou Eternal, disappoint me not, I bind me to thy
bidding;
   I will obey thee eagerly, as thou dost open up my
life."

Psalm 119:25-32

Why, it was the young man's current autobiog-
raphy! And God has continued to marvelously open
up his life from that day to this.
   Although scripture *is* inherently and everlastingly
relevant to the problems of life, there *is* one sense in
which we have to *make* the scriptures relevant, and
that is by applying them, by practicing their principles in our lives. Here, as an example, is an illustration involving the practicing of the truth found in
Mark 11:24, which reads, "I tell you, then, whatever
you ask for in prayer, believe that you have received it
and it will be yours." (NEB)
   As the mother of six children still "in the nest" I
find myself praying in the midst of problem situations
quite frequently. Many of my prayers are "asking"
prayers, because there is so much in which I need His
help as I go about my daily tasks. Most of all I need
patience in the midst of circumstances fraught with
all the pitfalls of impatience.

96

One day our four older children were in school, as usual, and I was at home alone with 'Guerite and Maria, who was then only ten months old. 'Guerite was in desperate need of a nap. She was distraught about something, however — I couldn't determine what it was — and wanted me to lie on the couch beside her crib, holding her hand until she fell asleep. That could have taken a long time, and I had other urgent matters to take care of — the little baby among them.

I can remember many times in the past when such incompatible demands upon my attention tore me apart with frustration, when the very necessity for communicating calmness and peace seemed to bring on a frenzy of frantic feeling of utter impossibility. But, on that day, by His grace, I was able to live in Him, and so found the solution to all problems ever present.

After making the family room as safe for the baby as I could (she had long since graduated from a play-pen), latching the doors, securing the gate across the stairway, giving her a pile of fascinating toys to play with in the middle of the rug, and committing her to the Father's care, I led my loudly protesting 'Guerite gently and lovingly upstairs, just as if I had nothing else to do. Putting her in her crib, I lay down on the couch beside it to hold her hand and satisfy her need for my attention.

Lying there with my eyes closed, I prayed about the situation in which I found myself. God knew all about it already, of course, but for my own sake I had to acknowledge it to Him. I expressed what I supposed must be His will for the upset child, that she become as peaceful and beautiful as He had created her in His perfection. He knew, better than I did, that she needed rest. And He knew the other things I needed to be doing. Giving the situation fully to Him, confident that He would do whatever was best, I thanked Him and said, "Amen."

'Guerite was still gripping my hand tightly, wide-awake and crying out from time to time. An unbeliever might have scoffed, "See, it didn't work. She's still wide-awake and determined not to let you go. Prayer didn't help."

That reaction would have been scriptural, all right. In James 1:6-7 (NEB) we read, "But he must ask in faith, without a doubt in his mind; for the doubter is like a heaving sea ruffled by the wind. A man of that kind must not expect the Lord to give him anything."

But I was not an unbeliever. I was a believer, concentrating on the promise of Mark 11:24. I had asked in faith, believed that He would grant my request, and had, in fact, already thanked Him for it.

To a believer, the space between sending a prayer and receiving the answer, however short or long the time may be, is a necessary space, a space in which faith becomes operative, a space in which *faith has to be the actual evidence of the existence of things not seen!* (Hebrews 11:1) The interval doesn't mean that God has not acted. He works His wonders in *eternity* and we have to exercise faith for them to unroll in *time.*

What need would there be for faith if we saw a thing the very instant we prayed for it? What need would there be for hope, for a thing already visible to us? "Now hope that is seen is not hope. For who hopes for what he sees? But if we hope for what we do not see, we wait for it with patience." Romans 8:24-25 (RSV)

In far less time than it takes to tell it, my child's crying had stopped and her hand was relaxed in mine. Her breathing was even and deep, her eyes softly shut in peaceful sleep. Once again, He had given His beloved sleep. The scriptural promise of I John 5:14-15

98

(RSV) was confirmed: "And this is the confidence that we have in him, that if we ask anything according to his will he hears us. And if we know that he hears us in whatever we ask, we know that we have obtained the requests made of him."

I am thankful for the little daily things that exercise and reward simple faith in prayer. I believe that the very same principles apply in situations where the interval is a matter of days or weeks or years instead of a few short minutes.

Occasionally there are things that happen to us to point up the meaning of scripture that had not shown its light to us before.

One evening my husband and I had gone out of town to attend a dinner meeting. Instead of leaving our teen-agers in charge of the little ones, as we did sometimes, we hired a babysitter to take care of 'Guerite and Maria and get them ready for bed. That left our teens free to finish their extensive homework and get in bed themselves at a reasonable hour.

When my husband and I arrived home at midnight, the house bore signs of recent and prolonged bedlam. Furniture was disarranged, toys were strewn everywhere, our teen-agers were frantically occupied with still unfinished schoolwork and the babysitter looked completely unravelled. Although the little baby was in her crib, she was fretting instead of sleeping, and our three-year-old was still on the rampage downstairs.

The sitter was apologetic as I handed her a check and my husband prepared to drive her home.

"I'm sorry about the mess," she said. "But 'Guerite didn't want to go to bed."

"Oh, that's all right," I lied. Inwardly I was seething. *What did she mean, "didn't want to go to bed"? Babies should be put to bed whether they want to go or not!*

99

As the door closed behind the sitter I ordered the big kids to their beds immediately, dumped 'Guerite unceremoniously into hers, *daring* her to get out of it, got the little baby to sleep with a few ounces of warm milk, and ferociously attacked the debris in the family room. The relaxing "evening out" had come undone.

The next night I was at home. But when bedtime came 'Guerite and Maria seemed to have completely forgotten their usual trouble-free, happy bedtime habits. The baby kept fussing in her crib — usually she snuggled down and said "nite, nite" as I went out. And 'Guerite kept getting out of bed and starting down the stairs, asking for milk or water or a teddy bear or a boat or a ball — Her bed was so full of *things* there was barely room enough for her when I tucked her in for what I hoped would be the last time *that* night.

Wearily flopping into my easy chair, I picked up yesterday's newspaper. The little baby started to cry louder, and I heard sounds indicating that 'Guerite was planning at least one more foray into the downstairs toybox.

Oh, no! I couldn't bear the thought of another trip upstairs. And I began to be very indignant toward the baby sitter we'd had the night before. It was all *her* fault. If *she* had taken proper care of the little ones, putting them to bed at the proper time and inducing them to sleep like good little girls, I wouldn't have to be suffering so now. I was really disgusted at *her* failure.

Well, maybe prayer would help, even if I wasn't in the mood for it. But I was certainly in the mood for a little peace and quiet. Maybe if I asked Him to bless the little ones with sleep He'd take care of it. He had done so at other times.

And so I pretended to pray. But the words didn't

sound right — and my voice, asking for blessing, was rasping with vindictiveness and anger. Of course the upstairs racket grew louder.

But in the instant that I pretended to ask God's help, in the instant that I took His name in vain, I realized something. I couldn't possibly ask His *blessing* on a situation that I was using for *blaming*.

"No man can serve two Masters — forgive us as *we* forgive —" Here was scriptural truth that applied to *prayer!*

At once, by His grace, I was enabled to forgive, to stop holding onto the unhappy situation that prevailed the preceding night, and, in the same instant to accept His forgiveness of my stupid stubbornness. I didn't even have to ask Him to bless the babies with peaceful sleep then. All was suddenly quiet.

The same light is related to the thought expressed in Matthew 6:22, and may be *the* clue to the failure of so many of our prayers: "If thine eye be single, thy whole body shall be full of light." Loosely paraphrased, it might read, "If your vision, your purpose or intention, be *one* (a unity, not a divisiveness), then your whole being may be flooded with light (with blessing)."

We do get what we *truly* desire when we have a pure singleness of mind.

A wife can effectively pray for improved financial circumstances for her family — but *not* if she persists in blaming her husband for poor business sense. A mother can pray for her child to become more orderly — but not if she delights in scolding him for sloppiness. A man can be blessed as he prays to be healed of a sinus headache — but not if he plans to use the headache as an excuse for not taking his wife to visit her mother. An employee can pray for a raise — but not if he wants an excuse for being ungenerous with

101

the needy. I can pray for ability to get my work done — but not if I want to complaint about how much I have to do.

I can even pray effectively *for* my children, and *with* them, *if* I am willing to grow. That's a truth that was clearly brought home to me one summer.

It was a day when one of the boys was supposed to be doing the breakfast dishes. He'd been dawdling over the same half dozen cereal bowls for about two hours when I couldn't stand it any longer. Several times I'd gently suggested that he stop playing with watermelon seeds, stop reading the newspaper, stop detouring from the sink to annoy his sisters, and get on with his job. The only discernible result of my reminding was my mounting blood pressure. I was beginning to lose all my patience and was about to lose my temper too.

It wasn't the first time such dawdling had occurred. His slowpoke approach to chores was one of those insidious, continual drippings of irritation that could eventually wear away the toughest rock. It was the summer when I had made a new commitment to Christ and I knew we couldn't afford to have daily crises over such trivial things. They interfered with abundant life.

When he finally dragged the dishwashing to a reluctant and unsatisfactory close, having wasted half his morning and all my energies for the day, I gave him a piece of paper and a pencil — an old trick that never had been worth much — and asked him to write down his problem about the dishes and then propose a solution that would keep us all happy. I must admit I was especially interested in a solution that would keep *me* happy.

He wrote something about how he hadn't been getting his allowance regularly and how he'd be more de-

102

pendable about his chores if he was sure of a regular allowance.

I didn't like what he wrote. It made me madder than ever.

He knew why he hadn't had his allowance regularly. We'd been breaking all records for staying "broke" that summer. But we both knew that he hadn't suffered for registration fees to go to summer camp or for a new bathing suit when he wanted one, or for anything else he really needed.

Swallowing hard I strode to the cupboard where we all kept our "allowance jars." I counted out the money in baby's jar and in my own. There was all of eighty-six cents. I thrust it at him.

"Here," I said. "Take what there is as an advance on your allowance for this week. I'll see that you get the rest of it when Daddy comes home. And don't let me catch you stalling at the dishes again!"

He refused the money. Bless him. He wasn't going to let me get by with an ordinary bribe. "It wouldn't be fair to the other kids," he insisted. "We all need our allowances, not just me."

Our impasse loomed more formidable than ever. But suddenly I remembered all that my new life was supposed to mean. This problem wasn't mine — or my son's. It was really His, and He'd tell us what the solution was if we'd only humble ourselves to ask.

Could we? I asked my son to accompany me upstairs, to the most convenient "holy ground." I asked him to kneel at the foot of my bed and I knelt beside him. It wasn't an easy thing to do. But it was the only thing to do.

"Dear Lord —" I prayed aloud as honestly as I knew how. "I don't know what to do about my son. And he doesn't know what to do about me. It seems that I'm forever nagging at him, and he's always dragging along as if he's trying to worry me to death. We can't go on like this. You've just got to help us. You have to make me the kind of mother I ought to be and help him to be the kind of person you've planned for him to be. He's so handsome, and so bright — and so bothersome.

"Forgive me for the wrong things I've done in rearing him, the times when I've been unloving because of the trouble he's caused me. Bless us both this day and show us the way out of our troubles. I think You would like for him to be helpful to me. I think he'd be happier if he did his work well and was proud of it. He can be so helpful when he wants to be."

"In Jesus' name, I ask it. Amen."

We stood up. I couldn't tell, at first, if praying had changed my son or not. But it had certainly changed me. I didn't feel vindictive any more, or resentful. I could understand, ungrudgingly, as I had not been willing to understand before, that a boy his age *did* need a dependable allowance. And I was cleansed of all desire to cement him in his wrong. I wanted to forgive — and to help. I had stopped being part of the problem myself. And I could speak to him with a new voice.

"I'm sorry about the allowance business," I said. "You really are helpful when you want to be, and you ought to have some income you can count on." It had occurred to me that there might be some change in the top drawer of the chest in my room and I opened it as we stood there.

"Look, now, I *want* you to have your regular allowance for last week, and this week's allowance in advance since you've had to do without for so long. And I can promise that from now on, no matter what, we'll have enough money to see that all of you get your allowances every week without fail."

104

I started to count out the change. $2.50 was the last regular allowance the older children had had. That gave them a dollar and a half for their school lunch money, a quarter for Sunday School and the rest for other needs as they arose.

I had counted out two dollars when my son interrupted. "That's enough, Mom. In the summer that's all you need to give us."

Wasn't he rubbing his knuckles against his cheeks as if something had changed within him, too? It looked like it. And I became surer as I saw how his behavior improved for the rest of the day.

I remembered the statement a professor at a small college made one day. We were in the midst of a committee meeting and were engaged in a heated discussion about some matter that needed to be settled. It wasn't the first time that that particular subject had been on the agenda.

Suddenly professor H——— stood up. "The last time this came up we had a frightful bicker. Is that still the procedure?"

We had all laughed because she had put her finger right on it — a frightful bicker *was* the procedure.

And I thought about the million and one things in our family life where bickering had been the procedure too, things that never got settled, that were the constant subject of nagging and complaint, things that should never have been problems at all. And I began to apply the power of real prayer to them. The results were always above all I could ask or think — when I prayed aright.

We've all known about the power of positive thinking for a long time. It's time for all of us to acknowledge the terrible prayer-killing power of negative thinking and ask of God:

Search me, O God, and know my heart!
Try me and know my thoughts!
And see if there be any wicked way in me,
And lead me in the way everlasting!
Psalms 139:23-24 (RSV)

With this hope in our hearts we are quite frank and open in our ministry. We are not like Moses, who veiled his face to prevent the Israelites from seeing its fading glory. But it is their minds really which were blinded, for even today where the old agreement is read to them there is still a veil over their minds — though the veil has actually been lifted by Christ. Yes, alas, even to this day there is still a veil over their hearts when the writings of Moses are read. Yet if they "turned to the Lord" the veil would disappear. For the Lord to whom they could turn is the Spirit of the new agreement, and wherever the Spirit of the Lord is, men's souls are set free.

But all of us who are Christians have no veils on our faces, but reflect like mirrors the glory of the Lord. II CORINTHIANS 3:12-17 (Phillips)

And we all, with unveiled face, beholding the glory of the Lord, are being changed into his likeness from one degree of glory to another; for this comes from the Lord who is the Spirit. II CORINTHIANS 3:18 (RSV)

When John the Baptist heard in prison about Christ's works, he sent some of his disciples to him. "Tell us," they asked Jesus, "are you the one John said was going to come, or should we expect someone else?" Jesus answered: "Go back and tell John what you are hearing and seeing: the blind can see, the lame can walk, the lepers are made clean, the deaf hear, the dead are raised to life, and the Good News is preached to the poor. How happy is he who has no doubts about me!" LUKE 11:2-6 (TEV)

New Flights:
Going Up

One Sunday morning I went to the nursery after church to get 'Guerite. As usual I stood talking to Virginia for a few minutes. When I was ready to leave I saw that 'Guerite had picked up a fuzzy dog from one of the baby cribs in the room.

Without gesturing at all I spoke in a normal tone of voice. "Put the doggy back in the crib, 'Guerite. Put the doggy back in the crib." Her mouth turned down in disappointment as she looked at me. She did *so* want to take the doggy home with her, but she had heard me.

Reluctantly, dragging her feet in their black patent leathers, and sniffling her disappointment, she turned and walked back to the crib to place the doggy in it, then came and took my hand to leave. I was pleased that she had understood — impressed that she had obeyed.

The next night 'Guerite was distressed because the cat had crawled under the rocking chair, out of her reach. She was crying, and the cat was meowing. 'Guerite lay down on her tummy and stretched her arms under the chair in a vain effort to grab the cat. I was about fifteen feet away, watching. I was tired and ready to get through with my chores so I could rest for

109

a while. 'Guerite was peering intently under the chair when I called to her, " 'Guerite, let's have a bath, let's have a bath."

I didn't gesture and she couldn't have been reading my lips because she couldn't see my face. But all of a sudden her crying stopped, she stood up and said, "Boa', boa,' " and ran to the toy drawer where she rummaged among her things until she found her little boats. Then she headed for the bathtub with them.

Later, after I had bathed her and loved her and put her to bed, the whole significance of the two episodes — the puppy in Sunday School and the boats for her bath — struck me with a positive assurance. His work, His healing work, in our formerly deaf child, was *complete!*

I was dazed. I could believe in the gradual improvement we had seen, but to come all the way to perfect hearing? That was beyond what I had really dreamed possible. And yet I knew His will for her was perfection.

More than a year has passed since that day. 'Guerite's audiogram still shows her to be a severely hard-of-hearing child. Her speech and her comprehension of the spoken word are still limited. But what kind of faith believes only when it sees? I must hold fast to the revelation of that day, remembering that whatever the evidence apparent to my ordinary senses, the promise of faith is wholeness. *His* work *is* done — now we must work and pray and have faith in order that His will might be made manifest in her.

"Lord, I believe; help thou mine unbelief."

On the evening that the revelation came to me I was filled to overflowing with thanksgiving. And an unexpected hymn kept running through my head: "O, for a thousand tongues to sing my great redeemer's praise . . ." I'd never seen the use of tongues before, for me.

But now I could understand. For how else could I ever thank Him enough? How could my own voice and ordinary words give sufficient praise? It could not. It would take all the music of creation, all the languages that had ever been, to thank Him — and even that would be inadequate.

A poem I had written once, a pagan poem, took on new meaning as I saw what it was really talking about. I had called it "Lament," but now I might call it "Discovery," or "Rejoice!" It went:

> Sweet is such a sour word
> Against the taste of You,
>
> Deep is such a shallow space
> Against my need for You,
>
> Steep is such a level plain
> Against the climb of love,
>
> Eons are as seconds to
> The hours we're apart,
>
> Where are the words that love can use
> To tell a lover's heart?

A few days later, still glowing from the experience of knowing how perfectly His work was going to be manifested in my child, I went to the library. I wanted to see what the circumstances were that caused Charles Wesley to write the words of the hymn of praise.

I learned that he had been critically ill, unable to take hold of either the physical healing or the spiritual comfort the love of God had for him. After a time of prayer, he heard a voice coming from somewhere outside his room. It said simply, "In the name of Jesus of

111

Nazareth, arise and believe, and thou shalt be healed of all thy infirmities."

The voice that spoke the words was the voice of Mrs. Turner, a woman too humble to confront the already famous clergyman with advice. But she had had a vivid dream, compelling her to climb the stairs and speak the words outside Wesley's door.

To Charles Wesley, it was as if God Himself had spoken. Suddenly all his distress and turmoil were gone. With a new, all-pervading peace, Charles opened his Bible and read prophetic words: "He hath put a new song in my heart, even a thanksgiving unto our God. Many shall see it, and fear, and shall put their trust in the Lord."

Later he wrote in his journal: "I now found myself at peace with God, and rejoiced in hope of loving Christ . . . I saw that by faith I stood; by the continual support of faith, which kept me from falling, though of myself I am ever sinking into sin . . ."

It was on the anniversary of this conversion that Charles Wesley wrote, "O, for a Thousand Tongues." One verse among the ones omitted from our Christian Church Hymnal, has come to be especially meaningful to me. It reads:

> Hear Him, ye deaf;
> His praise, ye dumb,
> Your loosened tongues employ;
> Ye blind, behold your Saviour come;
> And leap, ye lame, for joy.

We have seen that verse fulfilled, where someone has prayed.

Maria, once deaf, hears perfectly — because someone prayed.

'Guerite, once dumb, kneels beside her bed at

night, employing her tongue in praising Him, with a "Thank You, God, thank You, God, thank You, God!" — because someone prayed.

And Maizie, once so much worse than lame, leaps for joy — because someone prayed.

But what about the blind? I hadn't seen any formerly blind person beholding the coming of a Saviour— Or had I?

Surely I am the one who once was blind — blind to His power and His presence. And now I can see — I can behold my Saviour come — because someone prayed for me.

So let us all pray, let us pray for one another.

"And, lo, I am with you alway, even unto the end of the world. Amen." Matthew 28:20 (KJV)

Among so many, can He care?
Can special love be everywhere?
A myriad homes, — a myriad ways, —
And God's eye over every place?

I asked: my soul bethought of this; —
In just that very place of His
Where He hath put and keepeth you,
God hath no other thing to do!

Adeline D. T. Whitney

—NOTES—

—NOTES—

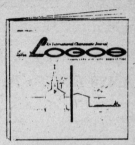

FREE
SAMPLE COPY
OF

LOGOS
An International Charismatic Journal

Worldwide Coverage
Feature Articles
Book Reviews
Trends

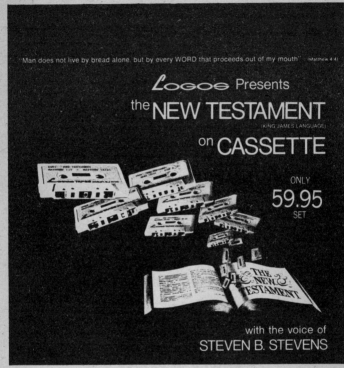

RECORDS

order from your local bookstore
or W.B.S.
Box 292
Watchung, N.J. 07061

SUGGESTED INEXPENSIVE PAPERBACK BOOKS
WHEREVER PAPERBACKS ARE SOLD
OR USE ORDER FORM.

A NEW SONG—Boone	AA3	$ .95
AGLOW WITH THE SPIRIT—Frost	L326	.95
AMAZING SAINTS—Saint	L409	2.50
AND FORBID NOT TO SPEAK—Ervin	L329	.95
AND SIGNS FOLLOWED—Price	P002	1.50
ANGELS OF LIGHT?—Freeman	A506	.95
ANSWERS TO PRAISE—Carothers	L670	1.95
ARMSTRONG ERROR—DeLoach	L317	.95
AS AT THE BEGINNING—Harper	L721	.95
BAPTISM IN THE SPIRIT—Schep	L343	1.50
BAPTISM IN THE SPIRIT—BIBLICAL —Cockburn	16F	.65
BAPTISM OF FIRE—Harper	8F	.60
BAPTIZED IN ONE SPIRIT—Baker	1F	.60
BEN ISRAEL—Katz	A309	.95
BLACK TRACKS—Miles	A298	.95
BORN TO BURN—Wallace	A508	.95
CHALLENGING COUNTERFEIT—Gasson	L102	.95
COMING ALIVE—Buckingham	A501	.95
CONFESSIONS OF A HERETIC—Hunt	L31X	2.50
COUNSELOR TO COUNSELOR—Campbell	L335	1.50
CRISIS AMERICA—Otis	AA1	.95
DAYSPRING—White	L334	1.95
DISCOVERY (Booklet)—Frost	F71	.50
ERA OF THE SPIRIT—Williams	L322	1.95
15 STEPS OUT—Mumford	L106	1.50
FROM THE BELLY OF THE WHALE—White	A318	.95
GATHERED FOR POWER—Pulkingham	AA4	2.50
GOD BREAKS IN—Congdon	L313	1.95

GOD IS FOR THE EMOTIONALLY ILL —Guldseth	A507	.95
GOD'S GUERRILLAS—Wilson	A152	.95
GOD'S JUNKIE—Arguinzoni	A509	.95
GOD'S LIVING ROOM—Walker	A123	.95
GONE IS SHADOWS' CHILD—Foy	L337	.95
GRACE AND THE GLORY OF GOD —Benson/Jarman	L104	1.50
HEALING ADVENTURE—White	L345	1.95
HEALING LIGHT—Sanford	L726	.95
HEAR MY CONFESSION—Orsini	L341	1.00
HEY GOD!—Foglio	P007	1.95
HOLY SPIRIT AND YOU—Bennett	L324	2.50
JESUS AND ISRAEL—Benson	A514	.95
JESUS PEOPLE ARE COMING—King	L340	1.95
JESUS PEOPLE—Pederson	AA2	.95
LAYMAN'S GUIDE TO HOLY SPIRIT—Rea	L387	2.50
LET THIS CHURCH DIE—Weaver	A520	.95
LIFE IN THE HOLY SPIRIT—Harper	5F	.50
LONELY NOW—Cruz	A510	.95
LORD OF THE VALLEYS—Bulle	L018	2.50
LOST SHEPHERD—Sanford	L328	.95
MADE ALIVE—Price	P001	1.50
MANIFEST VICTORY—Moseley	L724	2.50
MIRACLES THROUGH PRAYER—Harrell	A518	.95
NICKY CRUZ GIVES THE FACTS ON DRUGS —Cruz	B70	.50
NINE O'CLOCK IN THE MORNING—Bennett	P555	2.50
NONE CAN GUESS—Harper	L722	1.95
OUT OF THIS WORLD—Fisher	A517	.95
OVERFLOWING LIFE—Frost	L327	1.75
PATHWAY TO POWER—Davison	L00X	1.50
PENTECOSTALS—Nichol	LH711	2.50

PIONEERS OF REVIVAL—Clarke	L723	.95
POWER IN PRAISE—Carothers	L342	1.95
POWER FOR THE BODY—Harper	4F	.85
PREACHER WITH A BILLY CLUB—Asmuth	A209	.95
PRISON TO PRAISE—Carothers	A504	.95
PROPHECY A GIFT FOR THE BODY—Harper	2F	.65
PSEUDO CHRISTIANS—Jarman	A516	.95
REAL FAITH—Price	P000	1.50
RUN BABY RUN—Cruz	L101	.95
RUN BABY RUN—Cruz (Comic Book)		.20
SATAN SELLERS—Warnke	L794	2.50
SOUL PATROL—Bartlett	A500	.95
SPEAKING WITH GOD—Cantelon	L336	.95
SPIRIT BADE ME GO—DuPlessis	L325	.95
SPIRITUAL AND PHYSICAL HEALING —Price	P003	1.95
SPIRITUAL WARFARE—Harper	A505	.95
STRONGER THAN PRISON WALLS —Wurmbrand	A956	.95
TAKE ANOTHER LOOK—Mumford	L338	2.50
THERE'S MORE—Hall	L344	1.50
THESE ARE NOT DRUNKEN—Ervin	L105	2.50
THIS EARTH'S END—Benson	A513	.95
THIS WHICH YE SEE AND HEAR—Ervin	L728	1.95
TONGUES UNDER FIRE—Lillie	3F	.85
TURN YOUR BACK ON THE PROBLEM —Smith	L034	1.95
TWO WORLDS—Price	P004	1.95
UNDERGROUND SAINTS—Wurmbrand	U-1	.95
WALK IN THE SPIRIT—Harper	L319	.95
WE'VE BEEN ROBBED—Meloon	L339	1.50
YOU CAN KNOW GOD—Price	P005	.75
YOUR NEW LOOK—Buckingham	A503	.95

THE LOGOS INTERNATIONAL STUDY BIBLE

OLD AND NEW TESTAMENT: AMERICAN STANDARD VERSION
The world's finest Topical Analysis prepared by renowned scholars

WITH:--AMERICAN STANDARD TEXT (The Rock of Biblical
Integrity)
THE OLD AND NEW TESTAMENT
VARIORUM RENDERINGS*-- 150 scholars offer special
helps, suggested word trans-
lations, meanings.
TOPICAL ANALYSIS—A complete Bible analysis in one
volume.
CROSS-REFERENCES—100,000 cross-references.
INDEX, CONCORDANCE
MAPS

IN ADDITION:—THE LOGOS LAYMAN'S COMMENTARY
ON THE HOLY SPIRIT
With special reference index on every verse in the
New Testament referring to the Holy Spirit.

COMMENTARY EDITOR: **JOHN REA, Th.D.**—Biblical Research
Editor

CONTRIBUTING EDITORS: **HOWARD ERVIN, Th.D.**
RAY CORVIN, D.R.E., Ph.D.
ERWIN PRANGE, B.D.,Th.M.
DAVID du PLESSIS, D.D.
J. RODMAN WILLIAMS, Ph.D.
Fr. JOSEPH ORSINI, Ed.D.

FREE CATALOG
at religious bookstores
or
LOGOS BIBLE
185 North Avenue
Plainfield, NJ 07060

**Realizing the need for a quality but easily 'understandable HOLY
SPIRIT COMMENTARY, the editors combined their efforts in
supplying a verse-by-verse analysis of the New Testament.**

*Variorum renderings are alternate suggested words and phrases taken from
ancient manuscripts and offered as alternatives by leading Bible scholars.
Ancient Bible texts, their meanings, origin, and scholars' opinions are included.

1:8
partial
full size
sample
page

GENESIS
GOD'S WORK OF CREATION

God made the firmament, and divided the waters which were under the firmament from the waters which were above the firmament: and it was so. 8 And God called the firmament Heaven. And there was evening and there was morning, a second day.

9 And God said, Let the *a* waters under the *b* heavens be gathered together unto *c* one place, and let the dry *d* land appear: and it was so. 10 And God called the dry land *e* Earth; and the gathering together ters called he Seas: an that it was good. 11 said, Let the earth *f* grass, *g* herbs yieldi *and* *i* fruit-trees bear *k* after their kind, whe seed thereof, upon the it was so. 12 And brought forth grass, he ing seed after their trees bearing fruit, whe seed thereof, after th and God saw that it 13 And there was *l* ev there was *m* morning *n* day.

9
a Water, Ps. 95:5.
b Heaven, Deut. 26:15.
c Sea, Ex. 14:21.
d Land, Gen. 23:15.

10
e Earth, Gen. 2:1.

Var. Rend.—V. 9. heaven—heavens, R. V. 11. after their kind—in the several kinds thereof—*So throughout*. After its kinds, DR.; its kind, KA. V. 12. herbs—herb, R KA. their—its, R KA. trees—tree, R KA.

Var. Read.—Chap. 1.—V. 7. —misplaced, Di. De. Sept. Le GUN. place after V. 6.; cf. vs.

He knows All.—Job 23:24; Ps. 39:1-6; 149:4, 5; Pr. 5:21; 15:3; Is. 40:12, 14, 26-28; 46:9, 10; Jer. 23:24; Mt. 24:36; Rom. 11:33, 34; I John 1:5. **The Searcher of Hearts**—Gen. 20:6; Deut. 32:21; I Sam. 16:7; I Ki. 8:39; I Chr. 28:9; II Chr. 6:30; Job 11:11; Ps. 7:9; 44:21; 139:1-16; Pr. 15:11; 17:3; 21:2; 24:12; Jer. 11:20; 17:10; Amos 4:13; Mt. 6:4, 8, 18, 32; Lu. 16:15; Acts 1:24; 15:8; I Cor. 3:20; I Thess. 2:4; Heb. 4:13. **He knows Man's Condition and Needs**—Ex. 3:7; Deut. 2:7; II Chr. 16:9; Job 34:21, 22, 25; Ps. 1:6; 11:4; 33:13-15; 66:7; 103:13, 14; Is. 29:15; 37:28; 66:18; Jer. 32:19; Amos 9:2-4; Mt. 10:29, 30; I Cor. 8:3.

Foreknowledge of God.—Gen. 41:25-32; I Sam. 23:10-12; Ps. 139:15, 16; Is. 41:26; 42:9; 44:7; 45:11, 21; 46:10; 48:3, 5; Jer. 1:5; Dan. 2:28-45; 10:14; Mt. 6:8, 32; 24:36; 26:24; Luke 22:22; 24:27, 44; Acts 2:23; 3:18; 4:28; 15:18; Rom. 8:29; 11:2; Gal. 1:15, 16; II Tim. 1:9; I Pet. 1:2, 20. See "Prophecies concerning Jesus"—Gen. 3:15; "Prophecies and their Fulfilment"—II Ki. 17:13; "Election" and "God plans Man's Salvation"—Acts 2:40; "Foreordination"—Eph. 1:11.

He is Immutable.—Num. 23:19, 20; I Sam. 15:29; Job 23:13; Ps. 33:11; 102:27; Is. 40:28; Mal. 3:6; Rom. 11:29; Titus 1:2; Heb. 6:17, 18; Jas. 1:17.

He is Omnipresent.—Gen. 28:16; Deut. 4:35-39; I Ki. 8:27; II Chr. 2:6; Ps. 34:18; 139:7-10; Pr. 15:3; Is. 57:15; 66:1; Jonah 1:3, 4; Jer. 23:23, 24; Acts 7:48, 49; 17:24-28.

His Appearances to Men.—Gen. 3:8-24. To Cain—Gen. 4:6, 7, 9-15. To Abraham—Gen. 12:7; 17:1; 18:1-33; Ex. 6:3. To Isaac—Ex. 6:3. To Jacob—Gen. 32:30; 35:7, 9-13; 48:3; Ex. 6:3. To Moses—Ex. 3:4-22; 4:1-17; 19:19-24; 24:1-18; Deut. 34:10. To Moses and Joshua—Deut. 31:14, 15. To Solomon—I Ki. 3:5-14; 9:2-9; 11:9; II Chr. 1:7-12; 7:12-22. To Job—Job 42:5, 6. To Isaiah—Is. 6:1-8. To Ezekiel—Ez. 1:24-28; 2:1-9; 3:1-27; 8:1-4; 43:2, 3. To Daniel—Dan. 7:9, 10. To Amos—Amos 9:1. To John—Rev. 4:2, 3; 20:11.

63:1; Jer. 4:2; 9:24; 11:20; 1 14; Micah 6:5; 7:9; John 17:2 vealed in the Gospel—Rom. 1 3:9; II Pet. 1:1.

Goodness of God.—Ex. 33 II Chr. 5:13; 7:3; Ps. 25:8; 3 106:1; 118:29; 119:68; 135:3 33:11; Lam. 3:25; Nah. 1:7; Rom. 2:4; 11:22.

The Justice of God.—Gen. 45:21; Jer. 11:20; 14:23; 18: Zech. 9:9; Acts 17:31; Rom. is Impartial—No Respecter 16:19; II Chr. 19:7; Job 34 2:11; Gal. 2:6; Eph. 6:8, 9; spises None—Job 36:5; Ps. 2

He is Faithful who Promis 2:24; 6:4, 5; Lev. 26:44, 45; I Sam. 12:22; II Sam. 7:28; 2 9:7, 8; Ps. 18:30; 19:9; 25:10; 3:3, 4; 11:2, 29; 15:8; I Cor. II Tim. 2:13; Titus 1:2; I Pe

God is Long-suffering.—Ge 21; Ps. 86:15; 103:8-14; Is. 15:15; Ez. 33:11; Joel 2:13 17:30; Rom. 2:4; 3:25; 9:22; 3:9, 15; Rev. 2:21. **His Long** It was so with Pharaoh; wl hardened his Heart. Others Neh. 9:28-31; Pr. 1:24-27; 2 24:48-51; Lu. 13:6-9.

The Love of God.—Deut. Ps. 103:13; 146:8; Jer. 31:3; 16:27; 17:10, 23, 26; Rom. 5:5 2:4; II Thess. 2:16; Heb. 12:

and the day is now far spent. And he went in to abide with them. 30 And it came to pass, when he had sat down with them to meat, he took the ¹bread and blessed; and breaking it he gave to them. 31 And their eyes were opened, and they knew him; and he vanished out of their sight. 32 And they said one to another, Was not our heart burning within us, while he spake to us in the way, while he opened to us the scriptures? 33 And they rose up that very hour, and returned to Jě-ru'sȧ-lěm, and found the eleven gathered together, and them that were with them, 34 saying, The Lord is risen indeed, and hath appeared to Si'mŏn. 35 And they rehearsed the things that happened in the way, and how he was known of them in the breaking of the bread.

36 And as they spake these things, he himself stood in the midst of them, ²and saith unto them, Peace be unto you. 37 But they were terrified and affrighted, and supposed that they beheld a spirit. 38 And he said unto them, Why are ye troubled? and wherefore do questionings arise in your heart? 39 See my hands and my feet, that it is I myself: handle me, and see; for a spirit hath not flesh and bones, as ye behold me having. 40 ³And when he had said this, he showed them his hands and his feet. 41 And while they still disbelieved for joy, and wondered,

he said unto them, Have ye here anything to eat? 42 And they gave him a piece of a broiled fish⁴. 43 And he took it, and ate before them.

44 And he said unto them, These are my words which I spake unto you, while I was yet with you, that all things must needs be fulfilled, which are written in the law of Mō'sěs, and the prophets, and the psalms, concerning mɛ. 45 Then opened he their mind, that they might understand the scriptures; 46 and he said unto them, Thus it is written, that the Christ should suffer, and rise again from the dead the third day; 47 and that repentance ⁵and remission of sins should be preached in his name unto all the ⁶nations, beginning from Jě-ru'sȧ-lěm. 48 Ye are witnesses of these things. 49 And behold, I send forth the promise of my Father upon you: but tarry ye in the city, until ye be clothed with power from on high.

50 And he led them out until they were over against Běth'ȧ-nỹ; and he lifted up his hands, and blessed them. 51 And it came to pass, while he blessed them, he parted from them, ⁷and was carried up into heaven. 52 And they ⁸worshipped him, and returned to Jě-ru'sȧ-lěm with great joy: 53 and were continually in the temple, blessing God.

1 Or, loaf   2 Some ancient authorities omit and saith unto them, Peace be unto you   3 Some ancient authorities omit ver. 40

⁴ Many ancient authorities add and a honeycomb   ⁵ Some ancient authorities read unto   ⁶ Or, nations. Beginning from Jerusalem, ye are witnesses   ⁷ Some ancient authorities omit and was carried up into heaven   ⁸ Some ancient authorities omit worshipped him, and. See marginal note on ch. 4.7

ACCORDING TO JOHN

The Prologue

1 In the beginning was the Word, and the Word was with God, and the Word was God. 2 The same was in the beginning with God. 3 All things were made through him; and without him ¹was

not anything made that hath been made. 4 In him was life; and the life was the light of men. 5 And the light shineth in the darkness; and the darkness ²apprehended it not. 6 There came a man, sent from God, whose name was John.

1 Or, was not anything made. That which hath been made was life in him; and the life &c.   2 Or, overcame. See ch. 12.35 (Gr.)

LOGOS — $.95

THE NEW TESTAMENT

AMERICAN STANDARD VERSION

← *sample page*

THE APPROVED NEW TESTAMENT
~ NOT A PARAPHRASE
AMERICAN STANDARD VERSION
~ INTERNATIONAL EDITION